The Psychology of Twins
A practical handbook for parents of multiples

New Revised Edition

Herbert L. Collier, Ph.D.
Psychologist, family therapist and father of twins

www.TwinsMagazine.com
888-55-TWINS

The Business Word Inc.
Centennial, Colorado

TWINS® Magazine
The Business Word Inc.
11211 E. Arapahoe Rd., Suite 101
Centennial, CO 80112-3851
303-290-8500

© 2003 by The Business Word Inc.

New Revised Edition

All rights reserved. It is illegal under copyright law to reproduce this publication or any portion of it in any manner without written permission from the publisher.

This is a newly revised edition of *The Psychology of Twins,* first published in 1972, revised in 1974 and reprinted in 1980, 1982, 1985, 1998 and 2003.

Printed in the United States of America
10 9 8 7 6 5 4 3 2

Library of Congress Catalog Card Number: 96–79634

ISBN 0-9655442-0-6

www.TwinsMagazine.com
888-55-TWINS

The Business Word Inc.
Centennial, Colorado

Foreword

TWINS® Magazine is proud to take over the role as publisher of this new, expanded edition of Dr. Collier's intelligent guide to the world of twinship and parenting multiples.

As a parent of grown twins himself and a licensed clinical psychologist and family counselor, Dr. Collier is intimately familiar with the unique challenges, special joys and often-perplexing issues facing parents and caregivers as they live with twins and higher order multiples.

Parents who are raising twins will laugh—and perhaps grimace—while reading Dr. Collier's words of wit and wisdom as they recognize situations they, too, have faced. Some they're ashamed to admit they've dealt with badly. Others, they've handled well. From all, they've learned important lessons. This book will help parents, caregivers, grandparents and anyone else immersed in the world of twins and multiples to anticipate the next round of experiences—to know what lies ahead.

Dr. Collier's practice even today includes children who are twins and multiples, and families that have sets of multiples within them.

This handbook for parents of twins and multiples was first written by Dr. Collier in the mid–1970s when his twins were younger. Over the years, it has become known as one of the "standard guides" in the field. It is grounded in the real world of parenting, full of practical insights and advice, because Dr. Collier was "in the soup" himself. But its underpinnings are those of a practitioner of clinical psychology and family counseling.

The Psychology of Twins was last published in 1985, the year after TWINS Magazine was founded. Over the years Dr Collier has become well known nationwide as a leading speaker on the subject of raising multiples. He has been a frequent contributor to the National Organization of Mothers of Twins Clubs newsletter and has authored many outstanding articles on the subject of twin relationships and parenting multiples for TWINS Magazine, some of which have been included in this new edition.

Table of Contents

Foreword .... **iii**

Introduction **1**
   It all seems like a blur now 1
   Those tough early years 1
   Preparing for twins 2

1 Twinning: Some Basic Answers **5**
   Twintypes 5
   Identical twins 5
   How do you know? 6
   What are the odds? 7
   Carrying twins 8

2 Family Dynamics **10**
   Help! 10
   Pressures of a large family 12
   Father 13
   Working mothers of twins 16
   The mother substitute 17
   The effect of parental conflict on twins 18
   Divorce 20
   The singleton with twins 21
   A single older than twins 21
   When an older child regresses 23
   Pairing off 24
   A single younger than twins 25
   A singleton speaks out 26

3 Meeting Emotional Needs **30**
   Twins as individuals 30
   Who am I? 31
   Avoiding overdependency 33
   When one twin has a disability 34
   The smaller male twin 35
   The superior twin vs. the inferior twin 36
   Showing love 37
   Receiving love 38
   Acceptance 39
   Consistency 41
   Discipline 43
   The yelling mama 46

Communication	47
Bright, accelerated and creative twins	49
Hyperactive twins	50
Slow or retarded twins	51
When to call for professional help	54

4 Stages of Childhood 57
- What to expect from babies (birth to 6 months) 57
- ... from toddlers 58
- ... from 2-year-olds 59
- ... from 3-year-olds 60
- ... from 4-year-olds 61
- ... from 5-year-olds 62
- ... from 6-year-olds 62
- ... from 7-year-olds 63
- ... from 8-year-olds 64
- ... from 9-year-olds 64
- ... from 10-year-olds 65

5 Preschool Issues 66
- Feeding 66
- Feeding problems 67
- Bedtime 68
- Nap time 70
- Night fears 71
- Stimulation 72
- TV 72
- Toys 73
- Outdoor toys and games 75
- Destructiveness with toys 76
- Fighting, sharing, biting 76
- Language 77
- Stuttering 78
- Twin lingo 78
- Toilet training 79
- Thumb sucking 80
- Preschool 81
- Readiness for school 82

6 School-Age Issues 84
- To separate or not to separate 84
- What if one needs to be held back? 86
- Homework 87
- Grades 89

Morning problems	90
Chores	91
Twin allowances	93
Birthdays and presents	94
Bickering and fighting	95
Stealing	96
Lying	98
Sex interest and sex education	99
Sex play and masturbation	100

7 Preteen and Teenage Twins 102
Ongoing relationship building	102
Influence of the peer group	102
Who am I? Which one am I?	103
Outward signs of change	103
Inner problems	104
Promoting responsibility	106
Independence	107
School problems and teens	108
Driving and teenagers	109
Keep them busy!	109
Teenage boozers	111
The drug problem	111
Teen sex	114
Dropping out	114

Organizations 116

Recommended Reading 119

Introduction

It all seems like a blur now
When I asked my wife, Sharon, about sharing our secrets of twin parenting success with other parents, there was a thoughtful pause, a quizzical look and finally, her answer: "It all seems like a blur now. There was so much to do and so little sleep, it's hard to remember."

Of course, although Sharon and I find it hard to recall many of the episodes between our twins' births and their first couple of years of life, we do have albums full of photographs and some 8-mm film which vividly bring back the past! The only problem is that we were too busy during the first year to load the movie camera!

The recognition of Sharon's twin pregnancy created extremely strong, mixed emotions: surprise, delight, anxiety, terror and even anger at the thought of not being in control. But probably one of the most enjoyable times in our marriage was our anticipation of the twins' arrival. I recall that one of the ways we reduced our own anxiety and acted out our happiness and anticipation was to prepare. I built a hope/child chest in which we placed infant clothing, supplies and toys.

Those tough early years
After the babies' arrival, and especially because they were lightweight, there was the usual stress associated with no sleep, due to around-the-clock feedings every two hours. But the happiness and joy in watching Scott and Tracie develop was far, far more stimulating, challenging and entertaining than any television program or night out with friends.

I think that what helped us survive the tough early period was our ability and willingness to talk to each other, to share what was going on in our respective lives when we were apart, and our respect for ourselves and each other for what we were going through.

I personally never considered myself a psychologist in the family, nor was I ever treated like one. That is, I was never an "expert" in our home. There were frustrations and challenges, tough times, easy times and happy times. We were both very concerned about reinforcing each child's individuality. I think that our concern, our prayers and some luck have had a great deal to do with the fact that our twins, as well as our singleton child, have all developed into very warm, caring, sensitive, personable, independent individuals.

In addition, we believe the appearance of their younger sister, Lisa, was a great opportunity for them to focus some of their attention on her and compete for her attention.

We also thought that their being in separate classes, except for first and fifth grades, gave them a chance to really explore other relationships. We seldom referred to Tracie and Scott as "the twins"; we either referred to all three as "our children" or individually by name. As the older two grew and developed, strangers did not recognize them as twins. Their friends were aware of the fact, but did not make a big deal of it. Celebrating their birthdays together, within the family, was fun; however, they also had individual birthday parties with their friends.

There was the usual squabbling among all three of them that became irritating and boring at times, but usually they were easy to redirect. We tried to encourage them to identify what the conflict was all about and then try to solve it themselves, rather than our imposing solutions. I think our caring, love, respect and support for each of our three has helped them to feel confident and positive about themselves.

Scott and Tracie attended different colleges, Scott at Baylor University and Tracie at Westmont College. Lisa joined Scott at Baylor some three years later. We strongly believe those college years helped the twins to further elaborate their own individualities and identities. Fortunately, their graduation dates were separated by approximately a week, so we could be in attendance for both!

Today all three "children" are in their 30s, married and the parents of two children each. We still have strong bonds with all three and hear from them by phone. We are invited to visit them, and they come home and bring our grandchildren (none of whom are twins) on frequent visits and holidays.

The children have been a joyful blessing that neither of us would trade for anything in the world. So to those of you who are already parents of newborns, toddlers, preschoolers, grade schoolers, middle or high school students, rest assured that they will grow up. Enjoy each day and try to see parenting as a challenging adventure rather than drudgery.

And to you, the proud, perhaps surprised, possibly worried, expecting parents of twins—Congratulations! Hopefully you will have some time to prepare yourself for the babies' arrival.

Preparing for twins
Prenatal care is a must and in the case of twins may ensure against dangerous complications. But planning for the arrival of one baby or two should also include some type of how-to-do-it help, particularly if this is the first pregnancy (unless you are one of those rare individuals who has had a great deal of experience in dealing with newborn babies). You'll want to read books, like this one, that give

you a general look into your parenting future, as well as others that focus with more detail on your pregnancy and the birth and infancy of your twins. (See the Recommended Reading section at the end of this book.) You'll probably also want to take some kind of how-to class.

Local classes or demonstrations in many towns and cities, perhaps at the general hospital, will provide an orientation course for prospective new parents. These courses help young couples feel less nervous and worried about the approaching births. They inform the parents about admitting procedures and the regulations of the hospital, such as visiting hours. They may also provide helpful suggestions as to what kind of clothing may be needed, bedding arrangements, as well as various types of feeding methods, bathing, general care, and day-to-day management.

In some communities, the Red Cross, as well as Lamaze, La Leche League and others, presents excellent courses along these lines. My wife and I were fortunate enough to have attended this type of class for several weeks. It is extremely important for the fathers to participate, as it is difficult enough for a new mother to care for one baby let alone two. Although the newborn baby does not appear to be too interesting or challenging for many a father, time and an understanding of the baby's needs tend to make him feel more needed (which he certainly is), and to help him develop a closer relationship with the child early in its life.

Hospital or Red Cross instructors have frequently pointed out that the nursery for the newborns does not have to be costly or elaborate. Laundry hampers, dresser drawers and even boxes, when properly padded and blanketed, can do the job just as well as a frilly, draped bassinet. The important thing to remember is to meet the child's needs, both physical and emotional, and not to worry too much about unimportant details.

Living arrangements are sometimes difficult to manage in an ideal fashion. Twins placed in the same bedroom frequently manage very well. In other instances, they tend to interfere with each other's sleeping. They may have to be separated in order to assure sufficient sleep for each one (as well as for bleary-eyed parents).

When our twins were born, department stores in some of the larger communities provided what they called Twin Insurance. While this was a promotional and advertising ploy, it nevertheless could be helpful. Usually, it worked this way: Expectant mothers of twins (if they were lucky enough to know in advance) were encouraged to buy layettes and other equipment at the store, keeping the receipts for the items. Then, after the birth of the twins, the birth certificates were taken to the store, and all the single items which were purchased were duplicated free of charge. This could amount to a tremendous savings for parents at a time when expenses were going to be doubled.

Many Mothers of Twins Clubs have stockpiles of good, used clothing and a variety of twin baby equipment, including cribs, strollers and other expensive items. Since the use of these items is generally free of charge, it is helpful if you can donate some of your own twin materials upon returning the borrowed items, to keep the storehouse going. Also, baby furniture can be purchased cheaply through newspaper ads, various fund-raising rummage sales, and thrift shops.

Twinning

As parents of twins you will get plenty of questions from curious friends and relatives about the causes of twinning, the differences between twintypes, and the risks associated with carrying twins to term. Probably the same ones you already have yourself. So here are a few basic answers that may come in handy.

Twintypes

Identical twins occur after the fertilization of one human egg (ovum) by one sperm. In the course of cell division and development toward the embryonic stage, the fertilized egg divides, producing two independent entities (zygotes) having the same genetic composition.

In the case of fraternal twins, two eggs are released by the mother's ovary (or ovaries) instead of the usual one, and are then fertilized by two separate sperms from the father. Thus, their genetic makeup is no more similar than any brother or sister might be in the same family.

There is some evidence to suggest that in some pregnancies, one egg splits and then both products are fertilized by separate sperms of the father, creating a twin type that falls somewhere between identical and fraternal. This process is referred to as "polar body twinning". In order to diagnose this twin type, there needs to be extensive blood-typing of parents and twins. Nancy Segal, Ph.D., (professor of psychology and director of Twin Studies at California State University, Fullerton, and a frequent contributor to TWINS® Magazine) notes that additional research is needed to fully understand the frequency and nature of this type of twin.

Identical twins

Identical twins are always of the same sex. How often have those of us with different sexed twins been asked by curious on-lookers, "Oh! Are they identical?" One rather frustrated parent was known to respond, "No, they have different plumbing!"

Identical twins invariably look much alike with respect to all physical characteristics: hair texture, straightness or curliness, and hair color; skin color; eye color and shape; and general physical features. Blood tests reveal identical types of DNA and all the various chemical substances in the blood. Fingerprints, palm prints and footprints are very similar in their patterns, but it should be added that fingerprints of identical twins are never exactly the same. The pattern of the palms of the hands and soles of the feet are very similar but seldom exactly alike, yet those of identical twins are much more closely alike than those of fraternal twins. Ear shapes, too, are individual and distinctive, but always very similar in identical twins. In taste tests identical twins almost always react the same to the various chemical stimulants tested.

Sometimes physical traits appear on the opposite sides of identical twins. The hair whorl at the top and back of the head commonly appears clockwise on one twin, and counterclockwise on the other. One eye may be larger on one side of one twin, and on the other side of the other twin. Birth marks, too, can appear on alternate sides with mirror image twins. Likewise, one may be left-handed and the other right-handed.

In fact, "identical" is probably a poor adjective to describe twins from an appearance standpoint. Although genetically, with rare exceptions, they are "the same," identical twins can have small but significant differences, thought to be due to the splitting process, as the fertilized egg divides into two separate entities. Hence only one twin, for example, may have a cleft lip and palate, or spina bifida. The splitting process may also account for many minor difference, not all of which are birth defects.

Birthmarks, moles and dental patterns can be different, as can height and weight. There are even cases, explains Dr. Segal, in which identical twins are discordant for some diseases, such as epilepsy. As they grow up, it is not unusual for twins, regardless of twin type, to develop differently and to perform physical activities at different times.

How do you know?

Determining twintype is no simple matter. One common means for trying to do so is an examination of the placenta, but it is difficult to determine the nature of twin pairs on the basis of the placenta alone. Errors are often made, especially if it is assumed that one placenta proves twins are identical and that two placentas prove that they are fraternal. This does not hold true for a significant percentage of twins because it is possible for identical twins, if their separation comes at an early stage of development, to separate from each other with two different placentas, two outer bags (chorions), and two inner sacs (amnions), as happens with most fraternal twins. Moreover, fraternal twins may sometimes develop so close together that their placentas combine and appear as one. As many as 25–30% of twin pair with separate placentas may be identicals, and at least 20% of twin pair that have a single placenta may be fraternals. However, if there is only one placenta and clear evidence of only one outer bag, it is virtually certain that the twins are identical.

The most accurate tests to determine twin identity is DNA testing, since identical twins are completely alike in the hereditary make-up of all their tissues and of all their hereditary blood and chemical substances. The determination of twintype may be of critical importance should one twin need an organ transplant from the other.

What are the odds?
You have probably heard varying statistics regarding the frequency of twin births. Most of us would like a simple figure which we could remember and quote, such as 1-in-50, 1-in-77, 1-in-89, or 1-in-100. The incidence of twinning varies according to many factors. However, if we separate identical twins from fraternals, the statistics are more consistent. Identical twins account for between 3 and 4 out of every 1,000 births, regardless of other variables, whereas many factors affect the incidence of fraternal twin births.

For example, the incidence varies for different races. The highest rate of twinning is among African-Americans, with 1-in-70; for United States Caucasians it is 1-in-88; and for the Chinese, 1-in-300.

Studies have shown that the greatest period of twin production is between the ages of 35 and 40. A mother in that age group is about three times as likely to produce twins as a mother under twenty.

If the older mother is having her fifth child or more, she is more likely to produce fraternal twins than a mother under twenty having her first childbirth. Thus, whatever the mother's age, the more children she has borne previously, the greater her chances of producing twins in the next pregnancy.

Once a mother has borne twins, her chances of having twins again increase well beyond the average twinning rate. The odds of another twin birth for her have been estimated to be from three to ten times as great as those of a mother who has not yet had twins. Also, the chance of a twin repeat is generally much higher if the first pair were fraternals than if they were identicals. Thus, race, age and previous childbearing pattern all affect the odds.

Heredity is clearly a factor. The sister of a woman who has borne twins has about twice the average chance of producing twins in a given pregnancy. Mothers who are themselves twins have a greater-than-average chance of producing twin babies. Fathers, however, who are twins are hardly more likely to sire twins than are men in general.

Although the exact genes for bearing twins have not been identified, there seem to be inherited degrees of the twinning tendency. For example, in producing fraternal twins, the mother's ovaries may be unusually active, producing two or more eggs a month instead of the usual one. Also, the mother's womb may be especially receptive or provide a good environment in which twins can have a better opportunity to develop.

In producing identical twins, an inherited tendency for eggs to divide may result from something within the eggs themselves that causes them to divide easily in the early stages, or from something within the environment of the mother's womb that encourages the egg to divide; perhaps the father's sperm contains twinning genes that combine with the twinning gene from the mother to effect a division resulting in identical twins.

Thus, one must consider both hereditary and environmental influences for different types of twinning. In the case of fraternal or "two egg" twins, the determining influences are likely to be largely those which could enable a mother to produce more than one egg at a time. A conservative estimate of twinning as a result of the mother having been on Clomid is about five to eight percent; but it could be higher, according to one researcher who specializes in infertility issues.

Although much is needed in the way of factual material to explain human twinning inheritance, so far the authorities agree that the inheritance is complex and that any twinning genes probably come from both sides of the family. For example, in the case of fraternal twins, a woman's predisposition to produce two eggs at a time might result from the combined action of certain genes that she received from both her father and her mother. Yet, even given a wife who has this fraternal twinning tendency, it is not unlikely that the husband also plays a part in helping twins to be conceived. Such would be the case if his sperm are more than ordinarily active and long-lived, making it more likely that, if the wife did produce two eggs at a time, both would be fertilized.

In the case of identical twin production, the hereditary basis may come from both the male and the female sides. If a woman received "identical twinning" genes from both of her parents, the eggs that she produced would be more than ordinarily prone to split and form two babies. There is also the possibility that such genes might be carried in both the husband's sperms and the wife's eggs, and that when they combine in a given fertilized egg, identical twins result.

Carrying twins

The ability to conceive twins is only part of the whole picture. Carrying the twins through to a live birth can be a problem for some mothers. In the past, the mortality rate among twins was very high; a large percentage of those losses could be accounted for by the tendency towards prematurity in twins. Because of increased incidence of toxemia, fluid retention, abnormal presentation, complications of the cord, premature labor, and because of crowding and the relative decrease of the blood supply available to each fetus, perinatal mortality is also greater than in single pregnancies. Over the years, however, the mortality rate for twins has been steadily declining due to better prenatal care, improved obstetrical techniques, and added facilities for seeing more twins through their critical period.

The mortality rate also increases as the number of fetuses per gestation increases. The rates for twins, triplets and quads are respectively, four, eight and twelve times the rate for single births.

Also, one-third more of the second twins born were lost. There seems to be a tendency for the larger, healthier twin to activate his way towards the birth canal first with the weaker twin being left to follow, and perhaps encounter more complications.

Family Dynamics

Help!
The cry for help is almost universal upon the birth of twin babies! A new mother is sometimes overwhelmed, frightened and uncertain, and some mothers experience a temporary depression following the birth of any child. The help and reassurance of a mature, experienced relative or nurse may provide the needed moral and physical support she needs during those first few critical weeks.

Hopefully, a mother or a mother-in-law will be available for a period of time following their arrival, to relieve mother of the full responsibility until she can regain some of her strength. The proud grandmother can assist during the daytime so that mother can at least sit down and rest or catch the occasional catnap, which she will almost certainly need.

If there are older youngsters in the family, they can be trained to assist in the care of the twins in such a manner that they will not only feel useful but be useful, and because of this, feel that the twins are, in a significant sense, theirs. However, one must be careful not to make older children feel as though they have the full responsibility, lest they come to resent the twins.

Sometimes a high schooler in the neighborhood can be enlisted to assist with some of the routine kinds of chores (feeding, formula preparation, dishes, clothes, laundry folding, cleaning) so that mother can have a few quiet moments to enjoy the babies. Also, if someone can care for the twins at meal time, the rest of the family will have the chance to have a quiet, uninterrupted time together.

Those first few weeks, and sometimes months, are so hectic and tiring that I suppose many of us, when we look back, wonder how we made it through. The major problem is maternal sleep deprivation.

Taking care of twin babies is more difficult and complicated than the uninitiated individual might expect. In this case, the whole is definitely greater than the sum of its parts. With twins there is a very large "interaction" factor: in early infancy their cries awaken and agitate each other, so that one often has not one baby crying at a time, but two. Soon, they develop to the stage where they can move around in a playpen. Although they may entertain each other, which can result in perhaps less maternal attention than one might pay to a single child, they are also close together and, lacking coordination, can accidentally harm each other with their toys.

A certain variety is helpful. Young twin infants can often be placed in infant seats facing each other with overhead toys suspended on elastic straps within their reach. After short periods of this type of activity, they can be placed either in individual cribs or playpens, or attended to individually either for bathing or feeding purposes.

The challenges of caring for newborn twins are well expressed by this young mother: "I recently gave birth to boy/girl twins and am finding it quite hard to get a routine down and have time to complete my other obligations. I have been feeling anxious or nervous most of the time when alone with them, and restless and unable to sleep even when they do. Friends and family tell me it just takes time to adjust. However, as the novelty of newborn twins is wearing off on everyone else, I find myself alone with the babies more and more. Are these feelings normal? Is there anything I can do to make things go more smoothly? I feel as though they never will!"

This mother's reaction to her newborn twins is very normal. Her conscientiousness, care and concern for the babies obviously contribute to her anxiety and worry.

One of the most important needs for new moms is a support system. Her continued connection with her family and friends is crucial. Just having them available for her to share her worries will, over time, give her a sense of security. My own boy/girl twins just turned 34, and I am here to tell you that my wife and I can still remember those early worrisome days. But your confidence will grow as you realize that you are a good mom and that those babies are very, very lucky to have you.

In addition, here are a few specific things you new moms can do:
- Try to establish some structure for yourself each day, even if some days the best-laid plans will go out the window! Make the schedule flexible, but allot specific time for the babies' care, your own needs and then the housekeeping duties.
- Don't expect things to go smoothly or according to a precise schedule. Every day will bring unexpected issues but also many joys. Try to find some short relaxation exercises on cassette tape or learn to do some yoga or deep-breathing exercises to counter the stress and anxiety that you experience.
- Make time to affiliate with a Mothers of Twins Club or a TWINS® Magazine Pen Pal if at all possible. Knowing others who have experienced or are currently experiencing the same feelings as you will be an ongoing source of support.
- Plan some escape time. Mothers of newborn twins, because of the new and increased responsibility, and wear and tear on the nervous system, should be able to escape briefly during the course of the week. This type of encouragement I give to all couples with any number of children. A weekly outing does not have to be expensive. It can be a short walk, a drive to a shopping center to window shop, a hamburger out, a movie, or a visit to neigh-

bors, friends or relatives without the children. These types of outings seem to give new parents, particularly mothers, the necessary life needed to be able to carry on for another week. It is like getting your emotional battery charged, a battery which is drained very heavily in the course of the weekly duties.

Pressures of a large family

Statistics show that fraternal twins occur more commonly in families after several single children have been born. It is even likely that twins will find themselves in large families where there is more than one set of twins or other multiples. Many mothers, weary from the daily onslaught of demands by their broods, understandably feel frazzled, frustrated and fatigued. The mother always has the feeling that at least one child is not getting enough individual attention.

In those cases where singletons are older, they can assist and take turns in caring for the younger twins. Unless the children are all extremely close in age (like six under 6), generally there will be one or two older children whose aid can be enlisted in caring for some of the younger ones. Generally, too, each child does not demand and require as much attention as every other child. Many mothers of large families rely on the children to fend for themselves at a much earlier age, teaching the children maximum self-help techniques earlier than is usual in smaller families. Getting the children involved in outside activities where there is contact with adults, such as scouting and church groups, can provide parent-substitute types of guidance as well. Neighborhood teenage helpers and girls wanting baby sitting experience may be enlisted to help.

With a large family, the father may have to work longer hours or take two jobs in order to make ends meet. Thus, he may not be as available to emotionally give of himself to his children and to his wife as a father in a smaller family might. What we need to remember here is that in any family the amount of time we spend with any particular child is not as critical as the quality of the time we spend (even if it's only a few minutes).

It is much more difficult to take each child alone on outings, and it may be necessary to take two or three children at a time, while leaving the older children to care for younger siblings. In any case, father and mother have to work together very carefully and plan their strategies to ensure that one or the other of them is making some kind of significant and meaningful contact with each of the children during the course of the week.

Besides time pressures there are very real emotional stresses, like the feelings of isolation and insecurity that this young mom expresses so well: "I am the mother of 3-month-old twin boys and a 4-year-old son. I am very happy about having twins, but at times I don't believe I am coping that well. My husband works outside the home, and I stay at home with the children. Our families offer no support, and I have virtually no outside help at all. I feel very isolated and insecure; I feel as though I am going to cry half the time. There must be plenty of mothers who handle the adjustment just fine. Maybe I am expecting too much from people. I sometimes think I just wasn't cut out for this. Any advice?"

This woman has described a situation in which many mothers of twins can say loud and clear, "I have been there! It is tough, but you can survive!" Being a mother of twins without sufficient support can make one feel inadequate, frustrated, isolated, anxious and depressed. If this is how you feel, I suggest that you try to connect with a support group in your community.

Clubs for mothers of twins and multiples, for example, are available throughout the world. Their major goals are education and support. Their members understand what you are going through because they have been and are on the parenting firing line. If a club is not available in your community, check with your pediatrician or a community referral agency to see if you can connect, even by telephone, with other mothers who are in similar situations.

According to Jessie Groothuis, M.D., (a pediatrician at Children's Hospital in Denver and a frequent contributor to TWINS® Magazine, and a mother of twins), there is a nine times higher frequency of abuse in families with twins. When she talked with parents of twins and asked how they felt about having twins, initially everyone said they were thrilled, but probably because they believed that they were supposed to be thrilled. After she got to know them better, she asked the question again and only about one-fourth of the hands went up.

Dr. Groothuis strongly believes that fathers of twins need to be aggressively involved in multiple birth child care because there is a geometric progression of work involved with raising multiples. She advises that when anyone offers to help you, don't turn them down! Asking for help does not make you a "bad person" or "bad mother"!

Father
In any new family, the father should be more than just a provider of the shelter and bread. He needs to give of himself in assisting with the twins. He needs to learn to feel comfortable in holding and carrying the infants. The "football" hold (when you cradle the body of the baby on your left arm with the head in your left hand) frees the right hand for door-opening or other necessary activities. He needs to have enough experience changing diapers so that it becomes sec-

ond nature (and so that he doesn't turn green!). He needs to be involved in the nitty-gritty, day-to-day chores and in the fun of being a real parent.

I want to stress the importance of the father's role at this particular time of the children's life; it should include direct assistance as well as moral support. Because he doesn't have the physical closeness to them for as long a period during the course of the day, he may be willing to help out at night. Also, the father, who is out in the "real" world every day with adults and stimulating experiences, needs to take some time to discuss these things with his wife. His sharing of his own life, as well as his spoken approval and encouragement of her abilities in carrying through her own heavy responsibilities, can help to compensate a mother for her feeling tied down, fenced in or trapped.

His physical assistance in the care and management of the infant twins as well as other children is not only important but necessary. Caring for two babies is more than a full-time job for one person. A husband who refuses to participate in the care of an infant because he feels that it is unmanly or that it is not part of his role as a father is grossly uninformed and is missing a great deal in terms of parental responsibility and in developing a real feeling for his children and his wife.

With the birth of twins, an increasing financial responsibility may make it necessary for father to work more than one job. Yet, it would be better, if possible, to lower the standard of living somewhat, or to at least halt an increase in the standard for awhile, so that he could be physically present to help.

We live in an age of affluence, an age when many families feel the need for multiple luxuries, time-saving gadgets, etc. As a result, many fathers (and mothers) are working longer and harder hours to provide these for the family. Sometimes the father does not become as involved with the children as he should.

Father brings a variety of experiences into a marriage, depending upon his upbringing. Since our own parents are the models or teachers of our behavior, the father of the family will be better equipped if he had a "good father" himself. Hopefully, too, father has had an opportunity to experience a period of relative "freedom" prior to marriage so that he does not have to revert back to adolescence after he has taken on the considerable responsibility of wife and children. Ideally, by the time a man is married and has children, he feels secure as a person, confident in his role, and capable of giving. He has to be sensitive to the needs of others.

Many times, children's problems can be traced to a difficulty in their relationship with their father. Sometimes, father is aloof, detached, and uninvolved emotionally. Sometimes, he sees his role as a rather narrow one: that of provider. In reality, father has a very complex set of responsibilities, and plays multiple roles. He is likely to be the ultimate authority in the family, can be a teacher on many occasions, a leader, and a friend.

Some fathers feel that they cannot be both the authority and a pal. They feel that these qualities conflict and they fear losing control if they become pals to their children, especially the boys. If father has a good relationship with his children and if he has earned their trust and respect, then the children will probably try to please him and he will not need to fear "losing control."

Sometimes fathers are confused and guilty when it comes to their relationship with their sons. Fathers' and sons' interests may be vastly different. A father may be intellectually oriented and have little or no interest in sports, or he may be very sports-minded and find that one or more sons has little tolerance for athletics. Yet, this does not mean that they cannot learn to become involved with each other and have mutual respect. Father needs to provide opportunities for his children to develop many different skills. Even if he is uninterested in sports, for example, he can provide his son with sporting equipment and instruction through some other source to see whether this is something that his son would like. While he does not have to coach Little League ball teams, he can let his son know that he approves of what he is doing and encourage this kind of activity simply by being present at the games.

I had an opportunity of hearing the NBA player for the Phoenix Suns, Dick Van Arsdale (himself an identical twin), at a father/son meeting one night. He was talking about this very thing. He said in effect that, while his father was not particularly interested in playing basketball himself, he did provide his twins with a basketball and the hoop, and in effect told them to "go to it". His encouragement of them must have had a great deal to do with the fact that they both were very successful professional basketball players.

Those fathers who are not either gifted or interested in sporting activities can direct their sons towards Boys' Clubs, after-school activities, Little League baseball, and Pop Warner football teams, soccer, swimming lessons, gymnastics, horses, boxing, wrestling, karate, judo, etc. Obviously, no single boy will be interested in all of these activities but at least some exposure and some opportunity to be involved and to try some of these activities may reap rewards in the long run.

The father/son relationship is of critical importance in the boy's developing an adequate picture of himself as an emerging man; he gets a great deal of confidence from his relationship with his father.

Father's support, encouragement and enthusiasm about his son's emerging growth and skills provides a feeling of real confidence in a boy.

A father of twins often finds himself in a frustrating situation of having to meet the demands of two different personalities simultaneously. He often feels himself pulled in many different directions, and can become frustrated and discouraged. Yet, finding the time to spend in activities with the twins, together and individually, is of considerable importance in developing those feelings of uniqueness and individuality which are stressed elsewhere in this book.

The activities that father and his children become involved in do not have to be the kinds of things that the children themselves prize highly. For example, if the father has artistic interests, he can expose his children to the art museum, art shows, and other artistic endeavors. By sharing with the children at a level they can understand, he can give them some appreciation for the arts.

A bookish child might be encouraged to attend a football game with his father. Prior to the game, his father could briefly describe the game and try to impart some of his enthusiasm to the child so as to build up his curiosity and readiness for it. During the game itself, the various rules and techniques can be pointed out; the father's enthusiasm as well as the enthusiasm of the crowd may help the child to develop a broader interest.

Sometimes a father is "turned off" too easily by his sons' and daughters' lack of enthusiasm for participating in activities with him. He shouldn't give up. Of course, as the children grow older and acquire their own friends and interests, father and mother both may become "rejected" as a companion. Yet, in the long run, this is what we want: increasing independence of our children so that they do not need to lean on us throughout the rest of their lives.

Remember that the extra effort of a father to be present to his children does not go unrewarded, as this perceptive mother writes: "I am encouraged at the tremendously good effects my husband's spending of time with our boy twins individually and together has had on them lately! The twins seem to be developing more confidence in themselves and feel better about themselves. I'm finding my job easier and the experience has been rewarding and joyous to observe."

Working mothers of twins
Parents of families in which it is necessary for both the mother and father to work in order to make ends meet (which, with twins, can be difficult indeed) often express concern about the unhealthy effects that the mother's absence might have on the children.

Psychologically, it would be preferable for the mother to be with the youngsters during their very young and formidable years. After all, these are the months and years when the children's entire foundation for later life, the kind of persons they will become, the type of personality they will develop, is laid. It is very rare to find a "substitute mother" who will feel as sensitively towards the child as the child's own mother. It would also be unusual to find a baby-sitter who could fulfill all of the needs that children have. So, if mother does have to work, sometimes it may be possible for her to be gone from the home during the same time that the children are gone; or, if they are very young, the mother may work those hours when the father will be at home to care for the children. The latter may help the children to have better and more consistent handling, but the staggered schedules can certainly be a strain on the husband/wife relationship.

Mother has to be honest in asking herself the question, Do I really have to work? Is taking a job due to real economic necessity or is it to provide luxuries? Is it a permanent or only a temporary measure? Far too often temporary positions turn out to be permanent because of the desire for extra materialistic goodies. Some emotionally disturbed children, for example, state that their parents have been all too conscientious in providing "things," but have been short and sometimes even bankrupt in providing for the emotional needs of the children. Among those who remember the ravages brought about by the depression of the 20s and 30s, there seems to be a feeling that we don't want our children to be deprived of the things that perhaps we went without. Yet, some degree of self-sacrifice, or having to wait for and work toward something that we want, may be character-building. And those of our offspring who are provided everything that they want as soon as they want it may well be lacking in realistic values and moral fiber.

The mother substitute
Some mothers work because they enjoy working. They need the particular outlet and experience that work affords, and it is not just for economic reasons. These women are generally independent individuals who require a good deal of outside adult stimulation in order to function best. Their careers or positions meet special needs that tending youngsters can't. Thus, they make better mothers if they are not housebound, and their time with the children is more gratifying to them and to the children. As full-time mothers, they would be frustrated, unhappy and probably fulfill fewer of the twins' needs.

For those mothers who do work, the selection of good baby-sitters is extremely important. It is preferable to get someone who can come into your home to provide for a good continuity in care. This type of help is admittedly much more difficult to find than a day care center or a baby-sitter's house where the child is dropped off. Selecting someone who is mature and who has had some experience with youngsters is a must. One would want to know a good deal about the person's character, judgment and reliability. It will be necessary to outline very carefully what her responsibilities are and what you expect of her in the way of care for the children. In the case of twins, you should also share with her your feelings and ideas about how you want her to treat them—for example, as a unit or as two separate individuals.

Where it is not possible to have someone come into your own home, it would be wise to find out how many other children the baby-sitter cares for in her own home, and whether she seems emotionally and temperamentally capable of handling twins.

At home, the father can and must help in assuming some of the responsibility in the care of the youngsters during dinner and preparations for bedtime. Young twins demand a great deal from mothers and to a lesser extent from fathers, and the tired woman who, like her husband, spends eight hours on the job, plus the time for transportation, may not feel very receptive or giving at the end of the day.

The effect of parental conflict on twins

All parents experience differences of opinion, and have arguments about the way their children should be raised. The parents of twins sometimes find themselves in a more serious bind.

For example, one mother of twins recently stated: "My husband and I disagree horribly on raising our twins. He wants to raise them as 'twins,' and naturally I don't. He has read articles and has been to different discussions, but is still very strong in his feelings." More commonly it is the mothers who, down deep, are more concerned about perpetuating excessive preoccupation with twinship, while the father is more neutral. As one mother put it: "Why shouldn't I have some fun and get some recognition by dressing my twins alike? After all, I'm the one who does all the work."

Regardless of which parent takes which position, where parents are miles apart on their management plans and ideas, the result is a continuing, uncomfortable situation for the whole family. It also provides an excellent breeding ground for further trouble and complications as the twins become older and more sophisticated, and are able to take advantage of the differences between their parents, playing them against each other.

One of the most common conflicts arises when one parent, generally the father, is a rather rigid disciplinarian, has high expectations as to the children's conduct, and is very demanding and seldom rewarding. He is stern and unbending and apparently feels that if he shows any signs of weakness, or what he sees as weakness, he will ultimately lose control of the children. At the other extreme is the mother who is permissive, even inconsistent, "bending over backwards" to make allowances for the children's wrong-doings.

The chasm tends to widen between such parents because of their respective needs to compensate for what the spouse has been doing "wrong." The father becomes more rigid and more demanding and more punishing to make up for mother's weakness and permissiveness. Likewise, the mother becomes more permissive, more lax and less consistent in order to compensate for her husband's "lack of sensitivity." The twins find themselves in a situation where they soon learn to predict how the parents will respond to their behavior, and they begin, singly or together, to manipulate things so that they get their way the better part of the time.

Parents come into a marriage with long-standing ideas, attitudes and habits as a result of the conditioning they each received at the hands of their own parents. These attitudes and habits about how children should be raised are not easily changed, but can with assistance bend sufficiently to allow for compromises so that a more rational, healthy and consistent approach can be established. As compromises in management are put into effect, the result in the children's behavior is generally positive and encourages the parents to become more united.

We cannot and should not hope to protect the twins from all kinds of parental argument or conflict. The real world is full of conflict, and the family can provide lessons in how to minimize conflict. The children should be able to see that parents do have arguments and that they are resolvable, or that they can be ended through compromise or forgiveness, or some other type of problem solving. If a conflict is never resolved, if there is never an end to an argument, the anxiety is likely to remain, and this can have a psychologically damaging effect on the children. From a very early age, the children are aware of divorce, separation and break-up of families, and sometimes fear that this may happen to them.

In some instances, other types of conflicts arise in which a variety of alliances between the parents and twins can take place. For example, in the case of identical twin boys 9 years old, the father tended to identify very strongly with the "superior" of the two, while the mother took up the slack with the "inferior." The father was very pleased with the fact that one of the twins had developed interests similar to his own and that they could share so much time together in the enjoyment of these interests. They worked on model cars and airplanes together. They enjoyed attending sporting events together.

The other twin, more passive, perhaps the more sensitive of the two, found himself spending a great deal of time with his mother, who tended to encourage the identification of the boy with herself because of the father's outward rejection of him.

This arrangement, of course, did nothing for the relationship between the twins themselves, who had little in common and little tolerance for each other. In many ways, the parents were acting out their own marital conflict through the twins. Unfortunately, in this particular family, neither twin enjoyed the positive "blessing" of both parents and consequently both suffered for it. Only through professional intervention and working with all four members did the situation improve.

Another major conflict area in the management of twins concerns the need to bring father more actively into the handling and the responsibility for the children. As one frustrated mother noted: "This is not only difficult in our situation, but downright impossible. Not all of us are blessed with the beautiful 'give and take' marriages considered so ideal. Can't the children be made to realize this and understand it without impairing their emotional security?"

Why the father is not becoming involved makes a big difference when looking for a solution. Is it because of a demanding work schedule which results in his frequently being absent from the home? Or is it due to the fact that he is uncomfortable in assuming responsibility for the care of the twins? Or is it because of his deteriorating or poor relationship with the wife, which alienates him from the children?

Whatever the reason, he needs to know that his part in the raising of the children is extremely important and critical if they are to fulfill their emotional potential. Here, again, professional assistance may be needed to clarify matters. As part of the counseling, father's role in the family will be reviewed and an assessment made as to how his needs are being met, as well as how he meets the needs of the other family members.

Divorce

When the arguments and disagreements, the tensions and estrangement reach higher than tolerable proportions, one or both parents may seek separation or divorce. Couples often wait until this point to seek counseling or guidance, and then of course it may be too late.

The breakdown of the husband/wife relationship generally does not occur overnight. The marriage may have been a bad one from the start in that one or both of the members of the union may have been immature or unready for such responsibility. While there are many different reasons for marital disharmony, one of the generalizations seems to be that the parents cannot meet each other's needs.

Hopefully, marital counseling is given a fair chance to provide new tools for problem solving.

During the divorce process, however, the major psychological and legal concerns should focus on the children's best interest, not the selfish wishes or possessiveness of the parents. If the parents can produce their own parenting plan so much the better, but the paradox exists when they cannot agree, and become litigious and consequently forfeit much control to psychologists who do the custody study, to their lawyers and the judge, and ultimately complain about the outcome.

Most children will regret and complain about the parental separation, and hopefully parents will not consider separating the multiples as that would constitute another grievous separation, but their mental health can be protected by mature adult parents who cooperate in exchanging information about their multiples and are willing to share their time and responsibility with them. In this way there will be less opportunity for the children to lose trust in adults and develop their own emotional, personality, and or behavioral/conduct disorders later on.

The singleton with twins
The nontwin members of the family are sometimes in for a rough time. This need not be the case, however, if common sense prevails and if the principle of accepting each child for his or her own individual personality is the rule.

In some families, the single child may get short shrift because of all the attention given the twins. One must recognize that in any family where there is more than one child, there is going to be jealousy and competitiveness for parents' attention and affection. If twins receive the lion's share of the attention at the expense of the younger or older singleton, then those single born children have a much higher tendency to develop some kind of emotional or neurotic problem. The resentment will often not reveal itself openly, as it does in the child who fights, bites and throws temper tantrums. The child may reveal his resentment in more subtle, underhanded and "behind the scenes" ways. He may tease the twins, be overly selfish and prefer not to share his personal belongings with them; he may tattle incessantly or whine and otherwise kick up a fuss in order to divert some of the attention from the twins to himself.

A single older than twins
Where the single child is older than the twins, he is "up-staged" or displaced not just by one rival, but by two. One mother wrote: "Our single was prepared for a new baby, but never in our wildest dreams

did we think there would be two! So things have been difficult ..." During the period of the pregnancy, the ground work needs to be laid for preparing the single for the birth of the rivals (or rival, if the mother is unaware of the duo). This older sibling must feel that he will continue to be an important part of the family, and will have added status in the family because he will have some responsibility in dealing with the baby later and in the planning for the child now. For example, he can accompany mother on short buying trips, and may even have some say in the selection of articles of clothing or baby equipment. At least, this sib may be helped to feel that he is involved in the decision making.

Special attention should be paid to the relative bigness of the single child in relation to the smallness of a newborn. This child has to feel that there are large rewards in being big, in being a helper, and in becoming increasingly independent. However, nothing that we can do will completely erase all of the child's negative feelings about the "intruders."

During the hospitalization of the mother for the birth of the babies, special care needs to be taken to provide for as much continuity as possible in the daily routine of the single child or children. Thus, it is better to bring a mature relative into your own home to assist than to house the child elsewhere, unless the house is that of a close relative where the child has spent considerable time.

When mother returns home with the new bundles, particular care must be taken to include the single child as much as possible. Well-meaning relatives and friends can sometimes, without realizing it, have a disastrous effect on that single child as they overlook the older sib in preference for the new arrivals. Here, the mother and father can bring the single into the picture more actively by calling attention to the new role of big brother or sister, or by giving special attention in other ways.

In the day-to-day management of the children, it will be important, during those very brief moments when the twins are not needing something, to spend a few moments in giving the single child some undivided attention. This can be simply sitting and talking quietly, playing a game, or performing some worthwhile activity together, but it should be something that makes him or her feel like the most important person to you at that moment. During these times, let the child know that you recognize how hard it is not to be with you as much as he or she used to be; express your appreciation for the particular ways in which the child has been good or helpful.

When an older child regresses
It is not at all uncommon for the older, displaced child to return to earlier, more infantile behavior after the babies' arrival. For example, many mothers report that a child who has been successfully toilet trained once again begins wetting; a child who has stopped sucking his thumb once again begins sucking his thumb, and in general becomes more baby-like. This is not a conscious, carefully thought out plot on the child's part to upset the family; rather, it is an unconscious attempt to get more attention. He sees that the tiny babies require a great deal of attention because they do not have control of themselves yet, and wishes to return to that level so that he can have a closer relationship with mother. Therefore, a great deal should be made of the child's mature behavior, stressing all the time what a big person he is, how much fun it is to be big, and what the advantages are of being grown-up.

Here is where father can be a tremendous help. He can single out the older child and take him on special outings, which do not have to be lengthy and time-consuming. He can point out how great it is to be older because he gets to go out with dad and do special things, while the tiny babies have to stay at home because they still wet their pants. These brief outings can include something relatively small or special that the child enjoys, appropriate to his age level. For example, the two to three year-old might enjoy putting a penny in the gum machine during a trip to a grocery store. Older children can be rewarded for their mature behavior in other ways. Rewards do not have to be in the form of bribes, but can be remarks to the effect that the child is mature, helpful and special.

Sometimes mothers of twins report that the older, single child will not reveal the jealousy and aggression towards the twins, but toward one or the other of the parents, most often the mother. In this case, when the child vents his anger and resentment toward mother, she needs to allow him to do so—to get the anger out in the open, look at it, discuss it, and quietly reassure the child that he is important in the family and that he has a special place in relation to her. In other words, this is one of those situations where the mother has to do a tremendous "selling job" to reassure the child. I recognize that some children are less flexible in accepting situations like this, and consequently the efforts on the mother's part have to be much greater, more patient and sensitive, and more consistent.

Some mothers say that the single child, rather than acting out feelings directly, will tend to withdraw, shut himself off and fail to communicate in silent anger. Again, one has to recognize the child's need to express his feelings, and anything that can be done by the parents to encourage the child to "open up" will be helpful to him. Parents can facilitate the child's expression of his feelings with remarks like, "You seem very angry at me for bringing home these children." When the child sees that you recognize how he feels, it may be easier for him to bring out some of his feelings in the open. Some children fool themselves about the way they feel, and deny that they have any anger or bad feelings towards the younger children or the parents. By paving the way and letting them know that it is OK to be angry, and that you are willing to talk about it, you may make it easier for him to feel better.

In some instances, I have seen the older single child go overboard in paying a great deal of attention and perhaps even overindulging the twins. Recognizing the normal, underlying, mixed feelings that an only child has about being displaced, one must question whether this is not the type of individual who does a complete flip-flop in order to cover up her resentment. By being good, attentive, and protective of the twins, this individual child also gains a great deal of attention, support and commendation from the parents, so that in this respect her needs for attention may be met. So there is a very healthy element involved here, as well as a possible covered-over and denied type of reaction. In this case, it might be well, again, to pave the way for the child to express any underlying feelings of resentment by remarking that things are different than they used to be, "You must wish at times that you were the only child again."

Occasionally, one sees a family in which the older single child handles her competitive feelings towards the younger twins by attempting to excel, well above and beyond the call of duty, either at school, home or both. Such a one undoubtedly finds it difficult to come out with her true feelings about her younger competitors, and feels that in order to maintain her rightful position in the family, she will have to earn it. To gain the acceptance and love of the parents, she becomes a perfectionist, and in effect says, "Look at how much better I am than those younger kids!" Here is another case in which a child is likely to distort or misinterpret what we really expect or want from her. What we need to let her know is that we want her to be happy, well-adjusted and to feel an important part of the family, and that she need not drive herself beyond her own capabilities in order to achieve an unrealistic goal.

Pairing off
Occasionally we find that the older single child pairs off with one of the twins. This pairing off is really no different from what happens in families where there are nontwins but more than two children. It seems that when there are odd numbers of children, it is common for special subgroups or cliques to form. Sometimes these cliques remain constant and sometimes they change. They need not be

harmful unless two or more gang up on one of the others continually. In order to find ways to avoid this type of problem, or minimize it, a parent must understand the reasons for the subgrouping in the first place. An insecure or inadequate older child may find qualities in one of the younger twins that complement his own needs and that make him feel more adequate, independent and secure. If this is the case, the child should be helped to stand on his own two feet and not use the twin as a crutch.

Pairing off would be quite understandable for if the older child were a male, say 5 or 6, and the younger fraternal twin a male of 3 or 4. Any of you who have had experience with primary school–aged children realize how the sexes seem to stick together, how boys refer to girls as having "cooties" and other undesirable qualities that make them inferior. (At the same time, it is interesting to observe how children enjoy chasing one another and develop "crushes.")

Of course, not all the older child's favoritism may be due to insecurity. We should not forget that our children are just as vulnerable as we are in sometimes showing a preference for one or other of the siblings.

A single younger than twins
It seems to be more common to have an older child who finds it difficult to adjust to the birth of the younger children than to have a younger single child who has difficulties in relating to the older twins. However, many of the same principles outlined above apply to this situation as well. For example, twins need to be prepared for the arrival of the new baby, and parents need to plan ahead to avoid regression or infantile behavior on the part of the twins.

In our own family, this was the case. The twins were the only children until the arrival of the single child and received a great deal of attention not only from us, the parents, but from relatives and friends as well. Discussing the fun that they could have with a new baby seemed to arouse some degree of enthusiasm in them. Because they were only 2 years old, it was difficult for them to help in any planning, but they did, from time to time, indicate their willingness to share some of their more shopworn toys.

Following the birth of the single child, the twins continued to achieve individual attention from mother, grandmother, and father. They were taken on special outings on Sunday, and constantly received comments on their maturity, their "oldness," their bigness and the fun of being older. Also, they were both involved in caring for and helping with the new baby.

Because they were boy/girl twins, the girl twin and the single girl became closer to each other, which is understandable, although at times the boy twin and the younger girl had good times together. The usual complication arose when the three of them attempt to do things together; some pairing off seemed to be inevitable.

Occasionally, one finds the younger single child attempting to compete or perform tasks beyond his reach—those that come naturally for the older twins. Younger children may, for example, resent the fact that the older twins enjoy privileges and opportunities that they do not because of their age. They need to be reminded that they will have those same opportunities when they are older and more able.

Sometimes we find that we allow the younger child to do things that we made the older children wait until later to do. The older children resent the fact that Junior effortlessly receives nearly all the same privileges that they had to come by more slowly and painfully. This is common because parents tend to be more overprotective, anxious and unduly concerned about their first offspring and more relaxed and confident with those that follow, allowing the younger children more opportunities to do things that they want to do.

Discussing this situation very honestly with the older children sometimes takes the sting out of their resentment. We can tell them that we were more careful and more cautious with them and that we now realize that perhaps we did not have to be. Because they were successful in doing these things without getting hurt or causing problems, we feel confident enough to allow the younger child to do these things at a younger age. We can also stress that because the older children assist us, the younger child has the advantage of more supervision, more attention, more individual care; it is thus thanks to them that the younger child has more opportunities than they had being the oldest.

In general, whatever complication arises between a single-born and twin siblings, bear in mind the needs that all children have for individual attention, love, acceptance, consistency and communication.

A singleton speaks out
As a fitting conclusion to this chapter, I would like to quote from a teenage singleton who was asked to participate at a Mothers of Twins Clubs meeting and later made these observations. It may have a message for all of us.

"I was thrilled and surprised when I was asked to give my opinion as a singleton on a panel with twins. For many years, I believed that Mother of Twins Clubs did not recognize a single's needs. Now someone—me—could speak about the unique problems of a single raised with twins. But the panel was a big disappointment. I never got the chance to talk.

"My mother and I arrived at the meeting, and one lady eagerly turned to my mother and asked, 'Is she a twin?' 'No!' my mother said. 'Oh!' was her disappointed reply, and the lady turned to talk to someone else about twins. There was a buzz of voices in the room and the phrases I caught all evening were only about twins. One would have thought these mothers had no other children or interests. The meeting was then called to order and the guests introduced themselves by telling about their children—the twins' ages, weight, sex, and so on. It was a shock that several guests had to be reminded to stand again to tell what other children they had besides twins. One mother's remark especially cut. When asked if she had other children, she replied, 'No, thank God!' and everyone laughed.

"Next, the panel members were introduced and the questioning began. Just three questions were asked me about how it feels to be a singleton with twins in the family. There is no point, it seems, in singles being on a panel with twins. Mothers aren't interested in the singles' problems, and asked the twins on the panel silly questions. I felt as if I were merely a stage prop. One question asked me was, 'How much age difference is there between you and the twins?' Of what importance is that? They could have asked my mother just as well.

"I left the meeting so frustrated and angry. I felt that something should be done to help mothers of twins see what harm they may be doing their singles when they talk only of twins and twin problems. Singles are hardly mentioned in books about twins, because mothers just never talk about us. Yet, we singles must live and compete every day with twins.

"So how do we feel? Perhaps I can give you a fragment of the picture by answering some of the standard questions.

"Would I want to be a twin? I could have been happy as a twin in our family; but, no, I have never wished to be a twin. My basic goal in life is to be an individual—to be important as a person. The picture of twins that I got from that meeting of mothers was more like shadow play. I was not impressed, but disappointed in the trivia, the vanity.

"Would I like to have twins? Not just to brag or show off. Since when is having twins a talent?

"We singles so often hear the question, 'Do twins run in your family?' Just why is that so important? We don't understand why so much is said about it. Singles don't always understand grandma either, when she fusses over the twins and points out that they run on her side of the family.

"Should twins be dressed alike? No. Why should they? Why do mothers set their twins apart from the rest of the family? Isn't the family a unit? When my mother dressed the twins alike, it made us singles feel very out of place, especially at the club, family parties and family picnics where twins get more notice. We singles wonder about the constant talk about twins. We cannot understand the desire to dress twins alike when we know it draws attention away from us to Mom and the twins.

"Would I feel compared to twins? Yes, especially if they were the same sex as I. There has always been friction between siblings of the same sex, but the added attention and glamour of twins could only increase it. Therefore, I would probably develop an inferiority complex unless my mother made me feel just as special.

"How do we singles feel about club publicity pictures? We singles also like to see ourselves in print, but who gets into all the club pictures? Just the twins. This is a family affair? Isn't the club to help mothers raise all their children? At a 'family' picnic, the news photographer calls all the twins to the front where he carefully places each set of twins together, sorts them out by height, and snaps several pictures for the TV and the papers. We singles just stand back while our parents urge their darlings to smile at the camera. Then we listen while our mothers call all their friends and relatives to watch the rerun on TV, or watch for the paper. Do we love it? —About as much as you would love having one club woman getting all your club publicity.

"I wonder, too, how other little singles must feel about Santa at the club's 'family' Christmas parties. Wouldn't little singles resent Santa for paying more attention to twins? Doesn't Santa love all children? Wouldn't singles feel left out again when only twins get their pictures printed with Santa? What happened to the family part?

"Or how would I feel about twin fashion shows by the club? I would feel that this is unfair and would be frustrated if I wanted to share in the fun for the show but could not because my egg didn't split!

"What about twin birthday parties and publicity? I'd resent the photographers, the newspaper, my mother and the twins for making twins extra-special so often. It would make me indignant if my friends said to me, 'Oh, I saw your twins' picture in the paper again, and your mother's name. My, isn't it nice to have twins in the family?' Maybe not for the singles.

"How might singles feel about the extra attention that twins get in the stores, and the street? 'Oh, are they twins? How cute!' Doesn't this build hostility, not love, between singles and the twins? Does the single, then, act up to get his bit of attention? Wouldn't there be more family love if mothers did not dress their twins alike and if they were not noticed so often? If one twin gets a new dress, shirt, skates, why should the other twin get the same? We singles don't. Do we feel that this is fair? Not always.

"It's not easy living with twins. It's harder living with a mother who thinks twins are the greatest things that ever happened to her. Luckily, I have no such strong feeling except love for my own twin siblings. My mother doesn't try to get lots of publicity for herself and the twins, and I feel that this is important. We are each thought of as an individual, and I feel special, too. I hope that other singles with twin sisters and/or brothers are as lucky as I am."

Meeting Emotional Needs

Twins as individuals

If you have ever had a chance to observe newborn babies in a hospital nursery, you will notice that there is a great difference in their activity levels. Some babies are content to lie quietly, asleep or awake, while others thrash about very actively and make their demands known in a very loud voice. With twins, either fraternal or identical, it is very possible to observe different characteristics almost from birth. One twin may cry immediately upon awakening and demand, in a loud shriek, that he be fed; the other may wake up slowly, move about gradually, and work herself up to an increasingly loud demand for attention and food.

One twin will snuggle down in your arms very readily, and apparently enjoy being held, while the other may stiffen up and arch his back, as if to say, "Put me down" or "Leave me alone." Regardless of the reaction, each child deserves and needs to be handled. (You may have to "sell yourself," or over time convince him that this is what he needs. You should not, however, allow the child to reject you completely, no matter how independent he or she may seem. All babies need loving care and attention.)

Parents of twins are well advised to treat their twins as individuals from as early a time in their lives as possible. If you dress them differently and name them with nonrhyming names, older youngsters in the family, as well as relatives and friends, will think of the new babies as individuals rather than as some type of a cute, unusual unit. From infancy to about age one, there probably will be no irreversible damage done to the personalities of the twins if they are dressed alike. In fact, it may be difficult to dress them differently because of the vast number of look-alike gifts that well-meaning friends and relatives provide. (If you have a plentiful supply of identical clothes, alternate the days on which each wears an outfit.) The important thing is for mother, father, older siblings, relatives and friends to think of them and behave toward them as individuals.

If a mother of twins is a secure, mature and well-rounded individual who is happy in her marriage, and if she feels successful in her handling of other children in the family, she may not feel the need to capitalize on nature's accident to draw attention to herself, especially after the infancy period. It has sometimes been my impression, though, that mothers who are less secure, whose emotional needs have not been met in the marriage or earlier in life, are the ones who thrive on the attention paid to their twins. These become the "professional mothers" of twins, and are more likely to dress the twins alike to call attention to the twins and to themselves.

It is interesting to observe and listen to the rationalizations that these mothers offer for avoiding individuality in the handling of their twins. For example, much is made of the fact that a good deal of the clothing is provided for the twins (early in their lives) by relatives or friends: "What are you supposed to do?" Also, some mothers insist that the twins themselves have a strong desire to dress alike and to call attention to themselves as being especially different. Maybe so, but in this instance one must ask whether or not some conditioning hasn't gone into these patterns.

Toys as well as clothes offer the possibility of helping twins to function as separate individuals. As they grow somewhat older and become interested in toys, one of the concerns of the parents of twins as well as parents of non-twins is being "fair." Some parents, for example, feel guilty if they do not buy the same type of toy for toddler twins. However, there may be as great a reason to buy different toys as to buy the same toy. For example, instead of having two medium-sized green balls, one child may generally prefer a stuffed animal to a ball, but occasionally enjoys the ball, while the other generally prefers the ball. However, with a highly valued item, it may be necessary to have two to avoid unnecessary conflict. It is easy to see how, almost without realizing it, we can condition our children to develop the same interests by the way we treat them.

It is interesting how very early in their lives we can begin to notice differences in the children's preferences for different objects—toys, pans, cans, kitchen utensils, and so on—and different activities such as listening, observing or acting-out. They also differ in the way they relate with people. Thus, we need to provide a variety of opportunities for children to play, and generally experiment, with toys, utensils and other things; to listen, observe (even TV, selectively) and engage in other passive activities; to meet and interact with people of various ages.

There needs to be a balance between constantly making the children's environment interesting for them and encouraging them to seek out their own interests and ways to occupy themselves without parental guidance. Occasionally leaving children alone in their rooms and allowing them to develop their own resources for dealing with their environment is important. Too many people can never be happy unless they are constantly surrounded by other persons or engaged in one activity or another, and in general seem to be uncomfortable and restless when alone.

Who am I?

It may be fair to say that the majority of twins whom I have seen with some type of emotional problem have insufficiently worked-out concepts of themselves as persons. They do not know *who they are*. The failure to treat a twin as unique, as an individual, as a human being, has drastic and far-reaching consequences. Invariably, young parents of identical twins seem confused and uncertain as to how best to identify which twin is which. One young couple at a Mothers of Twins Club meeting stated that they were becoming increasingly alarmed because they could not identify any differences between their infants. It apparently had not occurred to them that some form of identification bracelet or necklace would solve the problem until their personalities had grown and unfolded enough to tell the difference. Recently, a mother of 14-year-old identical twin girls reluctantly confessed that her husband could still not tell them apart! He had continually, through the years, referred to them as "girls" or "Nancy and Sharon," never attempting to differentiate them.

Not only the parents but the twins themselves may have trouble differentiating themselves. Consider this case: "We are concerned with how our toddler twin sons view their individuality. If you ask each of them his twin's name, he answers correctly. However, if you ask each his own name, each will still answer with his co-twin's name. It's as if they see themselves as one. Is this common with twins?"

Depending on the age and the twintype of the children involved, this kind of behavior is not unheard of. However, according to family therapist (and identical twin) Eileen Pearlman, Ph.D., now is the time to start really looking at things you can do to enhance individualization. She stresses the importance of consistently calling each twin by his own name and very concretely pointing out, "Bobby, this is Jimmy." One must make sure that the children are addressed individually and not by a "unit" name such as "the twins." She also encourages parents to make sure that other people can tell their twins apart, by combing their hair differently or even putting name tags on them. Spending time with each child individually and using his name frequently should reinforce their individual identities. Family members and friends should be encouraged to do the same.

Imagine yourself with another person who always sits next to you and who is exactly like you in every respect and who may even be dressed in an identical fashion. This fantasy, to most nontwins, is rather frightening. We all want and need to be recognized for our own uniqueness, and we resent being compared to, or thought of as the same as someone else. Identical twins whose similarity has been exaggerated by dressing alike, engaging in like activities, and in sharing common friends, frequently attempt to compensate for the lack of individuality by exploiting the "secondary gain," in the way of attention and acclaim, that they get for being "freaks" of nature. Yet still they are not being appreciated individually for their own qualities, but only for the fact that there are two alike.

Family group activities are crucial in the development of healthy, normal children. In order to establish good communication skills, healthy attitudes, good ideals and standards, as well as a healthy self-concept and a feeling of self-identity, we must also learn to "individualize" our relationships with our children. This sometimes presents a real challenge when dealing with identical twins.

Beyond dressing twins differently, which helps them to differentiate themselves, it is very important to spend time individually with each child, particularly as each becomes more aware of what is going on in her environment. Research shows the development to be much earlier in infancy than used to be believed. I believe strongly that both mother and father should spend time with one child at a time. I do not feel that this requires long periods of time with each child, such as a weekend or a whole day (unless this is possible and comfortable for the individuals concerned). I do believe, however, that parents should take advantage of opportunities to be alone with a child, taking one twin on an errand or for a walk, reading a story, or just talking together—in other words, making the most of short periods of time when there will be no interruptions by other family members, so that the child has the complete and undivided attention of one or both parents.

Now, because twins are competitive, separating them long enough to get one of them alone with one parent can present some problems. A resourceful mother at a twins club meeting came up with an idea that has considerable merit. When both twins want to accompany father or mother on a brief outing, she flips a coin: one twin gets to go with the parent, and the other twin gets to keep the coin! Thus, with her young twins, the one who stays still has the satisfaction of a shiny penny. (I wonder how long that will last?)

As the twins become more verbal and can express themselves better, it is often surprising what they will share with a parent during these moments alone. It may not be necessary for the father or mother to say, "What's bothering you?" or "Tell me your problems." Just the fact that the child has undivided attention may prompt the share of some pleasing or troubling thing. This individualized attention promotes better communication with our children early in their lives. Patterns of receiving and sending feeling messages or attitudes, established early on, can prevent much misunderstanding and emotional turmoil between twins and their parents, and between the twins themselves, later on.

Avoiding overdependency
Extreme closeness of twins, particularly identical twins, can lead to some rather unique, sticky problems that interfere with the smooth

functioning and mental health of twins later on in life. Babies who are born at the same time and who have many identical experiences on a day-to-day basis and who spend literally thousands of hours together can become extremely sensitive to each other. In some ways, this may provide them with unusual capabilities as far as sensitivity is concerned, which need not be an unhealthy attribute. Certainly, most of us desire to develop feelings of comradeship, closeness, empathy and sympathy in ourselves and in our children.

However, overdependency becomes a problem when the children are so comfortable with each other that they apparently have no need for interpersonal relationships with other children their own age. Ways of preventing this are quite simple and inexpensive. Taking one child at a time for brief outings in a stroller or in the car can help him to realize that he is not an appendage or a part of his twin, but is indeed a real and separate person. Encouraging grandmother to keep one at a time for a weekend can also help. If the twin is always accompanied by his "shadow", he is very unlikely to develop the self-reliance and independence fundamental to good mental health.

If you are tempted to think that I am placing too much emphasis on following sound psychological principles in a child's infancy and early development, remember that personality characteristics are developed very early in a child's life. By the time she starts school, much of the ground work has already been laid.

When one twin has a disability
Because there is a higher incidence of prematurity among twins than among single-borns, and because there is a correlation between physical defects and prematurity, we can expect to find a variety of physical problems with twins. One would not expect, however, to find physical problems that are special or unique to the twin population. Fraternal twin pairs are more likely than identicals to have one who has a physical defect while the other is healthy. This situation can lead to several problems.

The twin with the defect may have a more negative concept of himself. Here, the parental attitude, if healthy, supportive and positive, will help the impaired child feel better about himself and will also influence the attitude of the healthier twin. The healthier twin's attitude will in turn have a positive influence on that of the peer group.

Helping the handicapped twin achieve a healthy self-concept will require a variety of tacks. An example: the boy in a pair of fraternal boy/girl twins, now nine years of age, was born with cerebral palsy, so that he is unable to coordinate his muscles smoothly. His sister rides a bike, swings and performs well, and with little effort, all the typical tasks requiring coordination. The boy stumbles and falls and experiences constant frustration at not being able to keep up with his sister.

To avoid the constant feeling of failure in comparison to a normal sibling, his parents placed him in a day environment with other cerebral-palsied children, where he learned that he could indeed compete with other children. In another direction, his parents made much ado about the fact that the boy had a good memory and surpassed his sister in table games. The confidence he gained from these different kinds of encouragement allowed him to try new things without fear of failure. In such cases, it is even more important that the two children be seen as individuals, rather than as twins, which carries the the subtle implication that they should be able to function equally well.

A twin who has a chronic health problem may both demand and require special attention from one or both parents. It is very difficult to know where to draw the line between providing realistic and needed care, and reinforcing a dependent attitude by rewarding the illness or physical symptom. Thus, there needs to be a balance between the attention given to the child's "sick" and "healthy" features. We should also keep in mind that the healthy twin will probably be sensitive to all the extra attention being paid to the less fortunate twin and may become jealous.

The smaller male twin

When a boy maintains at least equal growth or perhaps keeps a slight edge over his girl twin, problems relating to size differences may not arise. However, many mothers of twins are concerned when the girl twin consistently grows at a faster rate and even at the teenage period is larger than her male twin. One mother with two fraternal sets of boy/girl twins wrote that the fact that the girls far surpass the boys in size "really has a demoralizing effect on the boys."

OK, the girls are bigger than the boys. There is nothing that we can do about this from a physical standpoint. This problem is basically little different from those situations in which boys in general tend to feel inferior if they are smaller than their peers. "The Small Man Syndrome," as it is called in the literature, refers to the inferior, small male who attempts to compensate (or overcompensate) for his feelings of inferiority by outrageousness, overassertiveness, superficial superiority, vocal loudness and other alienating techniques. Other, and healthier, boys and men, with the help of their parents and siblings, learn to feel adequate about themselves, so that they do not have to use the compensatory or overcompensatory techniques that frequently lead to maladjustments.

The age of the stereotype in which the male is considered the superior in intellect, productivity, creativity, leadership, size, strength, etc., is drawing to a slow and painful end. If we accept individuals regardless of their sex, for their own strengths and weaknesses, then feelings about themselves may be more positive and they will not have the constant frustration about physical conditions over which they have little control.

The superior twin vs. the inferior twin

Many parents have observed that from a very early age one twin seems to assume a dominant or "superior" role while the other takes a more passive or "inferior" role. Any two children in a family may be very different with respect to dominance versus submission. However, if the relationship is an uncomfortable one for the twins, with one making all of the decisions, being outgoing, well-liked, friendly, popular, etc., while the other one is shy, withdrawn, and without friends, then some type of parental intervention is definitely indicated.

A total family effort may be all that is required. It may be enough that mom and dad make the effort to make the inferior child feel better about himself by paying attention to his strengths and complimenting him on his positive attributes. Encouraging the more confident twin to include his sibling in some of his activities, until the latter feels as though he can stand on his own two feet, may also help. But one should avoid putting too much responsibility on the dominant twin for fear that it may backfire. Teachers should also be made aware of the fact that you are concerned about the situation, in the hope that they may be able to provide some additional supportive measures.

If the problem goes well beyond the 6th grade, professional help should probably be sought. In my own practice, in addition to providing psychotherapy for the more passive, withdrawn twin, I have sometimes later brought in the more dominant twin as well, using a small group therapy situation in which both twins gain more insight into each other's strengths, weaknesses and problems, so that they learn to respect each other and themselves.

Sometimes parents, without realizing it, reinforce the aggressive twin's aggressiveness and at the same time encourage the passive twin's passivity. Parents can avoid a situation in which one twin feels grossly inferior to the other by paying attention to each twin's individual strengths, the strong points of their personality, their interest patterns and uniqueness.

Seldom are parents or teacher concerned about the extreme behavior of the dominant twin in its own right. Concern is usually focused instead on the effect this behavior has on the passive twin or on the effects that separating them (because of the dependency problems) may have. For example, one mother wrote: "My very shy twin became upset when separated from his confident brother. He could not keep up with the work. Shouldn't he be placed back with his twin?" We cannot expect more passive and dependent, inferior twins to gain any sense of strength and confidence if we allow them to lean on the superior twin. This is also a good example of when separation should take place earlier rather than later. The inferior, dependent child needs considerable love, reassurance and confidence-building experiences from both parents and teachers, and ideally from the other twin as well.

Interestingly, the more passive or dependent twin may, by displaying apparent helplessness, be more controlling and manipulating in the family and at school than is realized. It may be important here to obtain a professional consultation in order to distinguish controlling behavior from genuine fears or anxieties.

How a children feel about themselves is, of course, very important. A child who feels inferior will act that way, and people will respond accordingly. It is a vicious cycle. With encouragement, children can gradually learn to change their ideas or concepts of themselves, and once they do, people will start reacting to them in a way that they much prefer; this in turn enhances their concepts of themselves even further.

One mother wrote asking me if most identical twins tended to be opposite in their personalities. Twins, as a close pair of human beings, develop personalities that tend to complement or perhaps supplement each other just as married partners do. (The only difference is that the twins can't choose each other!) It is possible to have two identical aggressive twins or to have two passive identical twins. It is probably more likely, though, to find that their personalities do not tend to be exactly alike, but that over the years they have learned to accommodate each other, and to that extent their personalities are different. Because twins are so often in the spotlight at school, at home, and in the community, more attention may be paid to their personalities than to an individual child's. Simply remarking about a child's relative outgoingness or shyness may have a reinforcing effect. In this way, their respective personalities can become more divergent and more opposite than they might otherwise have become if not so much attention had been paid.

Showing love
Laying the groundwork for healthy, mature, well-balanced and well-adjusted twins involves giving and responding to a variety of their needs.

The development of emotions or feelings goes hand-in-hand with physical growth. How the child receives and expresses feelings depends to a large extent on the way the parents "do business" emotionally. Some experts feel that personality characteristics, including emotional qualities or traits, are inherited, or that at least predispositions to certain tendencies are inherited on a genetic basis. Others feel that the environment, or the day-to-day living circumstances, play a predominant role in deciding what type of emotional responses a child will make. Most recent research suggests a combination of these factors, with the lion's share of them probably being learned. Assuming this is so, then, we need to start responding to and stimulating our twins emotionally from the day they first come home from the hospital. We need to provide an atmosphere in which the children can feel loved and we need to show our love outwardly. In so doing, we provide a good framework for their feelings of security to develop and may avoid future problems.

Some parents report that they find it very difficult to show or express positive feelings outwardly; generally, these are parents who had little in the way of demonstrated love from their own parents. Outward signs of love include touching or caressing, hugging, kissing, etc. Parents who find it difficult to freely or comfortably express themselves in these ways often use a variety of means to avoid them, which may include a preoccupation with the physical surroundings, neatness, and general business to avoid becoming involved emotionally.

Parents who feel free in the open expression of feelings towards each other provide model behavior for twins to imitate and eventually learn, so that they in turn will feel more comfortable in this area of expression. Those parents who do not easily give demonstrable displays of affection, either towards each other or the children, can learn to do so. They should feel free to experiment with a variety of "loving" techniques. They may be surprised to find that the response from the children may be so great as to provide the necessary incentives to try again. These gestures may eventually become very natural and comfortable. Everyone needs to develop an individual style, and unfortunately a prescription for loving cannot easily be made.

Make the effort. One of the more important ingredients in the development of happy, well-adjusted twins is a large dose of demonstrable love between parents and from the parents to the children. Twins raised in such an atmosphere will likely feel more secure and happier, and will be less combative and competitive with each other.

Receiving love

Some mothers report that although they feel comfortable giving love openly, one twin tends to show a more ready acceptance of these expressions than the other. In this case, the mother and father both tend to show more love to the more receptive of the twins. Nevertheless, the more reluctant child needs to be given to emotionally, as much as the other; the outward signs of resistance, for whatever reason, are superficial at best. We cannot allow the one, seemingly rejecting twin to go without our love and so we need to continue to make every effort to break through the barrier.

Sometimes our twins, even in the case of identical twins, will distort or in other ways fail to receive the emotional message we try to send or will feel that we expect more than in fact we do. This is frequently seen in the child who feels unloved, rejected, or unfavorably compared to his or her counterpart.

There may also be errors or faults in the way the child sends emotional messages, or the mother and father may not be receiving the child's messages clearly. For example, one mother noted, "One of my twin sons (7 years old) and I don't seem to hit it off together. I love him dearly, and I know he loves me, but he favors his father. I have been away for six days now, and my husband, who is home with the children, informed me via the telephone that this twin is extremely unhappy because I am away from him and misses me much more than the other. Is this his way of showing his love for me, because he cannot show this love in any other way?" There is clearly a disparity between his not letting his mother pick him up and his strong reaction to her absence. At about 7 1/2, a child should have the verbal capacity to express some of those feelings, and maybe some brief quiet times with his mother, when these feelings can be shared more openly, would help get them both on the same channel.

Acceptance

"I like you for what you are with no strings attached" is a powerful statement and produces strong reactions. With twins it is especially important to show that each child is accepted for what he or she is, that we do not expect one to be like the other or to have similar traits, strengths or personality patterns. So often, problems in children can be traced to the very frustrating experiences they have in trying neurotically to meet what they see as an unreasonable parental demand.

Early in their lives twins may appear very similar. With time, their own unique personalities unfold. Parents respond to these developments and their responses affect the further unfolding. Each parent responds differently, and the children respond differently to each parent. A complex circular pattern emerges.

It is sometimes observed, and perhaps more commonly in one twin than in another, that one develops a way of behaving that is called "alienating." This behavior tends to turn parents off, make them angry, and generally make it difficult for them to like the child. For example, such behavior might include immature actions, demandingness, whining, dominating, selfishness, and overaggressiveness. Sometimes, these alienating techniques extend from the family into the neighborhood, and eventually into the school, so that the child is left with very few friends.

Unfortunately, children may have little insight into why they behave this way and may be incapable of making spontaneous corrections in their behavior to avoid constant frustration and disapproval, and the inevitable rejection by their peers and family. In such cases, parents must learn to avoid reinforcing those bad or alienating qualities, and the children need to learn to gain acceptance from others by using different techniques.

Consider the following illustrations of the circular pattern. A mother finds that she initially has the same positive feelings towards both of her twins, and then gradually notes some subtle differences in them, to which she responds accordingly. One mother noted that one of her twins was a passive, agreeable child who was easy to manage, got along well with other family members and with other youngsters. The other twin, however, became gradually more aggressive and negative, and threw temper tantrums. He engaged in frequent power struggles with her, thus threatening her authority. She slowly began to show more acceptance and tolerance of the twin with the positive characteristics and tended to reject the other.

When the mother realized what was happening, she began to feel guilty. The problem became so complex that the parents finally sought outside professional assistance. The therapist's job was to reverse the cycle that had led to the rejection and bad mutual feelings. Both twins needed to know that they were accepted, that they were important members of the family, and that they were both loved. The twin with the "negative" behavior also needed to know that while he was accepted, some of the things that he was doing were not. In fact, parental focus on his positive qualities soon reversed the negative cycle.

In a similar case, involving fraternal boy/girl twins, a father felt negative feelings towards his passive son and was more accepting of the aggressive daughter. The boy's passive, retiring nature presented a real threat to the father, who felt personally involved in the boy's lack of what he saw as suitable male traits. Without realizing it, very gradually, the father paid less attention to the boy, and the boy in turn became more isolated and more withdrawn. The relationship between the twins also became increasingly distant, and they were frequently very irritable with each other, with the boy striking out in an attempt to assert himself.

With assistance, the father began to accept his boy as a person and as a significant member of family, and then began working with him in male-type activities in which they could both have fun. As the boy began to feel that he had something good going with Dad, he gained more confidence. As a result, not only did he become more assertive at home, but he began to be more interpersonally aggressive at school and to achieve at a higher level.

In a pair of fraternal twin boys, a similar type of problem arose in which one of the boys developed an active interest that paralleled that of his father. As a result, a great relationship developed between the father and this son, while the other twin felt on the outside and rejected. He groped about for activities that he hoped would gain his father's acceptance, with little or no results. It seemed that everything that appealed to him repelled his father. The mother became the go-between or buffer and tended to make up for the father's lack of participation with this boy. Consequently, the boy began to identify with the mother's interests, and this presented other problems. Because he was becoming more and more feminine in his orientation, the family sought help.

The therapist found that the "maladjusted" twin indeed felt unwanted and unacceptable. After a few therapy sessions with the boy, the parents were encouraged to pay attention to and verbally reward the interests that the child did exhibit.

Eventually, the two boys were seen together, and it was possible to observe their interaction and to reassure them that they were both acceptable individuals with strengths. They were also able to see that each had weaknesses or was lacking in particular skills. The more passive twin began to grow more confident and to assert himself more openly. At the same time, the father went extra lengths to show interest in the boy's activities and to participate more actively with him.

In sum, children need to know that they have unique, positive attributes, that they each have things about them that we like and enjoy.

Consistency
Consistent handling of twins is one of the easiest things to advise, yet one of the most difficult things to maintain. If it is wrong for the child to walk across the kitchen table today or to jump on the sofa, then it will be wrong tomorrow, next week, next month and next year. In the course of the day, however, mothers soon become worn down, brow beaten and generally battle weary, so that they no longer have the stamina to stand up in a consistent fashion to the children's misbehaviors. Twins have been known to gang up against their mother and to undermine and weaken even a former Rock of Gibraltar. Even at

young ages, they can plot and plan devious strategies. Some of the plans are apparently not plans at all, but simply efforts to do their own thing, to assert themselves, to test their limits, or to reduce their boredom. I have been convinced, though, that in some cases and for whatever reason, twins consciously and with great effort and sensitivity plan psychological warfare strategies that would demoralize veteran guerrilla officers!

There have to be basic ground rules upon which both the mother and father can agree. Some families have very high standards with respect to what the children can do in different parts of the house (the living room, the family room, the back porch or the outdoors). The children have to understand and learn what is acceptable and where. In other families, there is much less concern about the carrying on of the individual children in any particular part of the house, short of activities that may be harmful to the children themselves or highly destructive to property. In any case, it really does not matter so much what the rules are as long as both parents agree on and maintain them.

Next, whenever an infraction occurs, it is necessary that the parents back each other up in confronting the children with their inappropriate behavior. If, for example, a mother punishes one or both twins and the father forgives, the one neutralizes the other; the children can be expected to be confused and undoubtedly one or both will perform the undesirable act again. It is surprising how many times parents undermine each other in front of the children, and then wonder why the children misbehave so badly. Consistency in handling really provides the twins with a good deal of security because they learn what to expect from the parents from one day to the next. Some of the most disturbed twins come from homes where the parents could never agree on child rearing methods or were so inconsistent as to completely confuse, bewilder and frighten the children. So-called "permissive" parents are frequently disorganized people who use their permissiveness as a rationalization for their lack of organization and consistency.

A good example of the importance of consistent handling of problems that arise early in life comes from a pair of identical twins, 4-year-olds, who during the course of the day ran their mother ragged by performing a variety of acts that were definitely "no-no's." These boys tended to act in concert, though one of them contrived most of the plots. Nap time was a disaster because they would demolish the room, crawl out the window, or put up such a ruckus as to make the whole idea of relaxing absurd.

In this case consistent separation was the cure, at least at nap time. One of the twins would sleep on a cot in the parents' bedroom.

The rest of the day's activities were somewhat more difficult to structure because they were together much of the time. However, the consistent reminder of impending separation, with the mother following through when it was appropriate, eventually led to more cooperative behavior. Also, the mother began to pay more attention to the constructive, cooperative efforts of the twins, and she began doing organized activities with them for five to 10 minute periods several times a day, which soon became more valuable to the twins than their misbehavior.

Discipline
Discipline, a highly controversial subject, has usually stimulated a great deal of discussion at most of the twin meetings I have attended. Discipline with twins is more complex and frequently more frustrating than with a single child.

Children need discipline to feel secure, to develop normally and to avoid feeling guilty. And they need discipline that is fitted to their own temperaments. Too many parents feel that they must use exactly the same disciplinary technique with both twins. Yet, we all recognize that children are different from each other, with different needs and different personalities, and that they react differently to disciplinary techniques. Thus, while fairness may require that we cut the cake or pie into equal proportions for each child, discipline need not be administered in the same way. One has to fit the disciplinary activity to the particular child. As the children become more aware of what is happening and remark about our being unfair, we have to explain how we are not in fact being unfair; because they are different, they won't always be treated the same.

One of the most difficult things for a gregarious child to handle is isolation or banishment to the bedroom, so that it may be an effective type of discipline for this type of child. A more passive or withdrawn child does not necessarily find it uncomfortable to be confined to quarters for a period of time. Thus, another form of punishment may have to be derived, such as a stern warning, or taking away a toy or activity.

For example, in a family where the fraternal boy/girl twins were quite different in their basic personality structure, it did not make too much sense to spank both of them for the same misbehavior. Spanking was not necessary for the girl because she was the more sensitive, thin-skinned and temperamentally tender, so that a brief talking to or brief isolation was all that was necessary. On the other hand, the boy, who was more aggressive twin, thick-skinned (and sometimes hardheaded), seemed to need a more dramatic and quick type of punishment to drive the point home. In this particular family, the parents felt very guilty if they treated the children differently in disciplinary matters, but they were torturing themselves unnecessarily.

In another instance where identical twin girls got themselves into trouble occasionally, identical disciplinary measures had only moderate success. Spanking had little desired effect either on the socially gregarious, outgoing, friendly and spontaneous youngster or on her sibling, who was more self-reliant, less gregarious and less assertive. By changing the discipline to fit the personality of the individual child, things worked out much better. The more gregarious, outgoing child was disciplined by isolating her in her room, with varying lengths of time suited to her "crime." The less assertive and perhaps mildly withdrawn child was not allowed the privilege of isolation but was made to face up to the consequences more directly in verbal discussion with her mother, followed by some household activity or chore.

It is important for the parents to be able to agree, or compromise, on some form of discipline for each twin which fits the infraction. By this, I do not mean that the father cannot use one kind of discipline and the mother another, but they should not undermine each other when they are carrying out their respective punishments. Both twins need to know what the boundaries are in their environment, how far they may go, and when they have met the limit of those boundaries. They also needs to know what to expect when they exceed those limits. The parents need to follow through to make sure their expectations are fulfilled. Children with inconsistently or poorly defined limits, or with no limits at all, will be emotionally confused.

Often, maladaptive or troublesome behavior can be avoided simply by not paying attention to it, that is, not "rewarding" it by making a big fuss. On the other side of the coin, when we pay attention to those things that children do that are good or improved or new and appropriate for their age, we let them know when they please us.

Because of the close proximity, competitiveness and the possible dependency, or sometimes hostile-dependency, that exists between twins, and because of the fact that they are together so much, they are likely to irritate or hurt each other occasionally. If the child performs a hostile act that is followed by a hostile act from the parent, say, in the form of an angry, uncontrolled outburst, the likely result is an increase in the angry child's already high level of hostility. When young children are fighting, it is necessary to step in and separate them and to isolate the offender, if it is possible to determine who that is. They should be told that when they can get along together, they can rejoin each other.

One of the best forms of discipline, of course, is to have children undo whatever wrong they have done. For example, when a young child takes a crayon and scribbles on a wall or a floor, he needs to know in no uncertain terms that what he has done is unacceptable. By taking a cloth saturated with cleanser, showing him how to cleanse his mistake away, even if you have to assist his hand in doing the job, may make more of an impression than a spanking. When a young child comes in from outdoors strewing her coat and hat helter-skelter behind her, "running the movie backwards" by having the child replace the garments, walk out the door and return and hang the items up properly serves to demonstrate the proper way of handling herself and her garments. The inconvenience of having to do this may help her avoid the unacceptable way the next time.

With young children, where infractions have occurred that are potentially dangerous or even life-threatening, disciplinary action must be very dramatic, to the point, and consistent. For the young child who does not understand verbal explanations, a sound slap on the fanny or on the hand may provide a dramatic reminder.

Parents ask the child specialists for the ideal or newest form of discipline to use in their family. My own feeling about the matter is that, in general, use what works. I do not think that spankings are always psychologically harmful. If they are administered in a timely, restrained and emotionally uninvolved fashion, they can be quite effective. In many cases, however, parents wait too long, store up anger, and then "explode!" Their anger and violent emotion is more harmful to the child than the physical hurt sustained.

Sometimes, especially frustrated parents will complain that no disciplinary action they have used, or that I have previously suggested, has been effective. In nearly every one of these cases, I have found that the discipline has not been tried over a long enough period and that it has not be conducted in a consistent fashion. Sometimes, when a parent goes from one form of discipline to another in a random fashion, the child becomes confused and angry and refuses to comply with any of the methods.

I also like to stress that discipline is only one side of the coin. The other side is continually building a positive relationship with the child so that he will want to do things to please us. Thus, when we do have to use disciplinary action, the relationship does not fall apart nor is there any serious breach. I cannot stress strongly enough the need for positive feedback. We all seem to be very tuned in to those things which our children do wrong, and we are all too quick and critical in terms of letting them know. How often do we, in the course of a day, let them know what they have done to please us? Perhaps a harassed mother will say, "There is not one darned thing that kid has done all day to please me or make me proud of him." In this case, I think she needs to refine her observation techniques so that she can find some little bit of behavior worthy of positive comment.

In some instances, an overly active (or hyperactive) child does not respond well to most forms of discipline. The problems associated with hyperactivity will be discussed later in this chapter.

The yelling mama

"I am really pretty good now about controlling my shouting, and my twins have commented on it," writes one mother. Often mothers say rather sheepishly: "I find myself yelling at the children far too much, I think." If the truth be known, I suspect that most mothers, being human, have varying degrees of built-in tolerance for frustration just as do other human beings. So, when their frustration level is reached, one way of blowing off steam is to yell.

Twins are more likely to push mother's vocal buttons than a single. Their tendency to jointly continue trouble, or avoid responsibility, frustrates and angers the harassed mother. Many mothers say, "They don't hear me or respond unless I yell." In some families the whole tempo or pitch of verbal communication is higher because of this need to get a point across. Some busy mothers give barrages of orders but get no response from the children. Children learn from very early on to "tune you out." Although most mothers are uncomfortable with yelling, and I don't know of many children who enjoy it, a louder voice, repeated commands and nagging can become a lifestyle.

Some psychologists believe that yelling is harmful to the child because it interferes with the mother/child relationship, and the child may learn to fear mother's sometimes violent verbal outbursts. Others feel it is just a useless and ineffective means of communicating. One psychologist I know broke several mothers of the habit by using a rather powerful and, some feel, sneaky technique. He had the children keep a small notebook in which to record the number of times per day that their mother yelled and the incidents that caused her to yell. It had a beneficial effect in several instances. Not only did mother become more aware of what she was doing, but the frequency of her yelling decreased considerably. The children themselves gained some insight into what they were doing to stimulate and encourage mother's yelling.

I believe that yelling has its place in family life, just as much as whispers, sidelong glances and other forms of communication. But it should be reserved for those special occasions when it is truly appropriate, when there is a need to punctuate one's message with a form of exclamation mark! A more personal and effective approach for general use is to maintain eye-to-eye contact (with a normal voice level) when giving the children directions or asking for assistance. Obviously, you can't do this if you insist on delivering commands from the other end of the house.

Communication

Communication is a very complex topic, about which much has been written. Communication involves the sending and receiving of messages. Good communication between persons requires mutual understanding, the ability to listen, the ability to hear what other people say, as well as the ability to express oneself so as to be understood by others. It also involves a certain amount of candidness or honesty in expressing oneself. Usually we think of communication in terms of the spoken word, but we also communicate in many nonverbal ways. A shrug of a shoulder, a lifted eyebrow, a turned down mouth, a sigh, a grimace, a stamping foot, a slammed door—all communicate some kind of meaning or feeling to us.

Within a family, the parents are the models for the development of communication skills. How they communicate with each other has a profound influence on the children. How often have you heard your twins playing your roles? How often are you embarrassed at seeing yourselves as they see you?

Communication, however, is not just for parents. The whole family needs to talk and all family members should be encouraged to be honest with one another without becoming combative or overly defensive. I know a family with twins who set aside time one evening every week—which they called "Tiger Time"—when the children could complain about things that they didn't like, about parental demands, unfair treatment, rivalry, etc. Sounds like a good idea? Beware: Not all parents have broad enough shoulders, big enough egos, enough confidence, or the maturity to be able to withstand some of the onslaughts from their children. Some parents who have tried this approach report becoming very angry and defensive, shutting off the meetings before the children could relieve themselves of all their built-up frustration and anger. Still, families need to talk, and they need to do so honestly.

The communication or sharing of feelings is very important. Where else is it safe or socially approved for children to express themselves but at home? Is it not better for them to blow off some steam, express some of their anger at what is happening to them than to hold it in? Better to talk at home than to develop some psychosomatic problem (such as an ulcer), explode at school (which will interfere with relationships there), or act out problems in an antisocial way that will bring the sky tumbling down on them and their family?

Communicating or expressing emotions is necessary for good mental health. All of us, perhaps, are like tea kettles bubbling away on the stove, building up a certain amount of steam as a result of frustrating or unhappy experiences. Like tea kettles, we need escape valves so that steam can get out instead of causing us to "blow up." In some families, parents are reluctant to allow children to express their anger openly. Many times it is mistaken for rudeness, snottiness, insubordination or lack of respect!

True, at times, it is difficult to draw the line between the honest expression of frustration and anger and the downright provocative act designed to anger a parent. Sassy or disrespectful remarks could be handled by saying something to the effect, "I don't talk to you that way, and I surely do not expect you to talk to me that way. If you have something that is bothering you that you would like to talk to me about or if I have upset you in some way, I will be happy to discuss it with you. But we are not going to get anywhere if we sit here and call each other names or insult each other." Banishing children to their rooms or becoming counteraggressive, doesn't really address the problem.

Sometimes the communication pattern between twins can inhibit the proper development of more general communication skills. Twins, being very close to each other, generally develop special communicative techniques very early. We need to make certain, though, that their exchanges are understandable by people outside the twinship. Several mothers of twins have written that one of the twins speaks for both, so that the more passive may be quite late in developing language or in asserting himself. One mother reported that her less active 5-year-old twin communicates with his sister but won't talk to others. Because her speech is more easily understood than his, she acts as interpreter.

The following steps may be helpful in facilitating communication skills:
- Dilute the relationship between the twins so that the more passive child will have to talk and will have an opportunity to express himself independently with other children
- Encourage verbal behavior by initiating conversations
- Reward independent verbalizations by praising them and calling them to dad's or others' attention
- Consider putting the twins in separate classes at school.

If the problem persists to school age, we want to be certain there is no mechanical (speech) problem interfering with the child's development; a speech evaluation would be in order.

Bright, accelerated and creative twins
Occasionally, the parents of identical or fraternal twins feel that one or both of these children are exceptionally advanced or bright for their age. Their impressions are often based on their knowledge of child development and their comparison of the twin, or twins, with other siblings, neighborhood children or relatives. They begin to suspect that their twins are particularly bright when they show quickness in motor skills, such as turning over, sitting up, crawling, and walking; when they express complete thoughts or carry on mature conversations earlier than most; or when they appear to be reading earlier than expected. Very often they contact a psychologist to confirm their suspicions when the children are between 2 and 6 years old.

Developmental or intellectual evaluation of young preschool children, however, should probably be reserved for cases in which the parents have questions about methods for dealing with an accelerated child, or about possible placement in a school with an enrichment program. To evaluate a child's IQ simply for comparison with other children or to inflate our own egos does not seem particularly worthwhile.

Many parents, of course, do have genuine concerns about whether they are "doing the right thing" in handling and managing their bright twins. In some ways, it is as much of a challenge and hardship to deal with an exceptionally advanced child as it is to deal with a retarded child. Parents who lack higher education may feel ineffectual, inadequate or incapable to meet a bright child's needs. Often these fears are unfounded, and all they need is the reassurance that their judgment and common sense in managing the children are enough.

Many educators recognize that some children are ready to learn complex symbols earlier than others, and this is why special schools are set up for the early training of gifted youngsters. Yet, keeping in mind individual differences in growth, maturity, social and intellectual rates of development, we should not jump to conclusions about our youngsters.

Some mothers are baffled or bewildered by 2-year-olds' recognition of a supermarket item or other frequently advertised goods from television commercials to which the children have been exposed. The fact that the children have been able to attend, comprehend and recognize these symbols in a different context suggests that they are alert and responsive and *perhaps* gifted. With the advent of television and the massive stimulation that very young children receive from it, many children learn to recognize symbols, even in the form of words, very early.

Other signs of brightness include constructive imagination, where the child will take some relatively raw material and construct something that appears to be the product of a much older child. Abstract thinking is another sign of possible advancement. It is one thing for a child to recognize objects, such as a doll or a table or a dog. It is more advanced and difficult for a child to recognize classifications of animal, vegetable or mineral; kinds of action, such as running, walking, or talking; or concepts such as largeness and smallness, inside and outside, top and bottom. The size of the vocabulary itself can sometimes be one of the best single measures or estimates of intelligence. Thus, young children with a large vocabulary that they use appropriately may indeed be very intelligent offspring.

In the case of fraternal twins who are obviously much more advanced and accelerated than their co-twins and other peers, we need to provide appropriate stimulation and encouragement for both twins. An average child in a situation like this often feels grossly inferior in comparison with the brighter twin. Again, we must recognize individual differences and accept both children for what they are, unique individuals. Parents should direct attention and approval towards their unique features to counteract feelings of inferiority on the part of the average twin. Unfortunately, in some families where intelligence and achievement are highly valued, a normal, average child often feels rejected.

Hyperactive twins
In recent years, a great deal has been written about children who are overly active, have short attention spans, are easily distracted, who act very impulsively, are irritable and irritating, and require constant supervision because of their poor judgment. These children are often thought of simply as troublesome or bad, or as being behavior problems. Generally, when they begin school, they experience difficulties learning because they cannot settle down and pay attention long enough to absorb new material. Some of these children have trouble learning the concepts involved in reading, spelling and arithmetic. Others do not seem to have difficulty learning, but their behavior is a disruptive element, at home and in the classroom.

A medical doctor finds nothing organically wrong with the child. Special psychological-educational measurements are available to identify particular learning disabilities. While we have had many of these measures for several years, and while we have been able to diagnose many of the problems, there has not always been a large enough number of sophisticated, well-trained educational specialists to do remedial work in specific deficient areas. Physicians have found that special medication will help some of these children operate more calmly, have better attention spans, and consequently be able to learn more easily. Experts disagree on the advisability of using such medications. The additional fear of drug abuse frightens some parents from using the medication, even when it is legitimately indicated and highly advisable. I have myself worked closely with several pediatricians and family doctors in cases where they have administered medications to hyperactive youngsters. I have been impressed with very dramatic improvement in some children. When using these medicines, it is important to check carefully with the physician so that the proper dosage and optimal effect can be achieved.

In any case, the environments and routines of hyperactive children should be simplified as much as possible to avoid overstimulation. Where possible, bedrooms or play areas should be painted a neutral color, without bright, stimulating wall coverings, toys and so forth. Classroom environments may be customized for these children: the desks face blank walls, or the children have their own cubicles, so that there is a minimum of contact from their peers and a maximum opportunity to focus on their work. At the same time, these children, like all children, need to be involved in those kinds of activities and exercises, usually outside, that allow them to expend a good deal of their energy. And when they are inside they need the calming influence of the soft-spoken rather than the screeching parent. I realize that this is much easier said than done!

One hyperactive twin can keep the whole family in constant turmoil. Parents feel very frustrated because they cannot help the child and angry because of the constant annoying behavior. Needless to say, normal co-twins take quite a beating, and frequently find it difficult to be tolerant of their hyperactive counterpart. Where both twins are hyperactive, parents really suffer. The twins seldom quiet down, except for very brief periods of time, are constantly into things, may be up and down at all hours of the night, and generally wear the parents down to such a point that by the time they seek professional help they are literally frantic. The interaction of two hyperactive twins creates such bedlam in some families that if separation is not possible, at least occasionally one or both must be placed outside the family for periods of time so that parents can recover and renew their strength!

Slow or retarded twins
Studies have shown that the incidence of retardation and physical complications is higher among prematurely born youngsters. We also know that twins are born prematurely more often than singletons. Insufficient nutritional supply before birth and complications during or immediately after birth, such as lack of oxygen to the brain, can result in some form of brain damage.

Slow development is usually easier to spot in a twin than a single because of the constant comparison with the other twin. Mothers who are with their children many hours of the day and night generally have good judgment as to when something is wrong. The family doctor or pediatrician is a good person to consult about your observations. Many parents, and occasionally doctors, will discount a child's slow development because of the tremendous variation in individual growth rates; the hope is that the child will eventually catch up. With twins, however, comparison is ever present, constant and ever nagging.

Periodic developmental evaluations by a trained psychologist can assist the doctor to determine the child's current level of development. The first evaluation serves a base against which subsequent evaluations, at six months or a year, can be compared.

Infant developmental tests evaluate the child's physical coordination, motor skill, perceptual and auditory acuity, and the beginnings of personal and social awareness. As the child grows older (towards the age of language development), the tests are more heavily weighted toward verbal behavior. Developmental or intelligence quotients are measures only of a child's current efficiency. No test can pretend to measure capacity or potential. Although a good test will measure what it is supposed to measure and obtain the same approximate score today, tomorrow and next week, scores should not be considered permanent or unchangeable. Children do progress unevenly, experiencing both plateaus and accelerated upswings. Also, some important characteristics are not directly measured by these tests, such as relative alertness, degree of responsiveness to examiner and environment, and the display of appropriate emotional signs.

There are many levels and kinds of retardation. If one or both twins is slow or retarded, parents generally want to know and should know what has caused this retardation to assist with future family planning. Many cases of retardation result from accidents prior to, during or after birth. However, if there is a chance that the defect is due to some genetic or inherited disorder, parents should seek genetic counseling to establish an exact diagnosis, if possible, and to assist them in making decisions about future pregnancies.

Fortunately, special education resources are available in many public schools for the majority of slow or retarded children. Some of these children can succeed in regular classes but require more time, more repetition and a greater degree of patience from parents and teachers. Such youngsters can eventually be taught a trade at a vocational high school, job training center, or vocational rehabilitation center, and can be largely self-sustaining. Many of them, however, if placed in normal classrooms, have few opportunities for success in competing with their peers. They need specially trained teachers to assist them in maximize their skills. In many communities, they are taught within the public school system, but in special classrooms. Here, the emphasis is on helping the children to become self-sufficient in meeting their own physical needs. Vocational workshops or other "sheltered" workshops may be available to further train these children as they go into the teenage period.

Where both twins are slow or retarded, the burden on parents is heavy. They have to be patient, repeat directions, spend a great deal of time not just with one, but with two. The emotional turmoil and frequent depression experienced by parents of one retarded children are worse where both twins are retarded. They must support each other and avoid blaming themselves or each other. They can overcome their sometimes profound feelings of guilt by participating in retarded children's organizations and other parent support groups.

When both twins are retarded, they are not as likely to experience the severe feelings of inferiority or failure that one retarded child might. They provide companionship for each other which a single child who spends hours by himself lacks. Where one of the twins is retarded and the not, there are likely to be different problems, as you might expect.

The slow twin needs the parents to establish realistic goals that are not be too hard or impossible to attain, but not so easy as to keep the child from attaining maximum growth. We need to become increasingly sensitive to the slower twin's emerging skills and interests, and comment favorably so as to encourage further growth and development. We need to help the slow twin, through evaluation and remedial work, to strengthen any weak areas and capitalize on all strong points. Learning will come in small increments, which should be recognized and praised. To avoid unnecessary comparisons, the twins should not be encouraged to participate in all of the same extra-curricular activities. Yet, this does not mean that they could not both be in scouting, for example. They could be in different dens or troops or, if the slower one is well enough adjusted and not overly sensitive, they could be in the same group.

Healthy parental attitudes about each child's uniqueness will be picked up by the children, and hopefully by their peers in the neighborhood. Nevertheless, neighborhood children may at times be very insensitive and even cruel to a slow or retarded child. There is a risk of developing secondary emotional problems as a result of prolonged frustration at not being able to compete in a normal family or class, or from being teased or berated for needing special attention. Therefore, we need to work constantly at being aware of and countering such influences.

When to call for professional help
Twins are probably no more likely than any other combination of children to develop problems that interfere with daily activity and smooth functioning. However, in my experience, I have seen more identical twins with problems than fraternal twins. Identical twins frequently have similar kinds of emotional difficulties, although there are exceptions to this.

For example, a few years ago, a 7-year-old identical girl twin developed an extreme concern about her clothing and would insist on it having as little contact with her body as possible. She insisted on wearing clothes which were much too large for her so as to minimize the chances of close body contact from the clothing. Because the parents could not correct this symptom—which was beginning to interfere with her daily living pattern, making her tardy for class, keeping her from school, and generally making her a very irritable child around the house—they brought her in for consultation.

The other twin was affected by her sister's irritability, and they eventually had to have separate bedrooms, but she was not otherwise affected and did not develop the same problem. With treatment, the symptoms gradually subsided to the point where they were no longer "neurotic" or interfering with her daily life.

A 10-year-old male identical twin was seen for general irritability, underachievement, temper tantrums, negativism, and a number of other disturbing characteristics. He had assumed the role of the more passive or "following" twin, while his brother was more aggressive and had fewer difficulties in adapting to home life and school routines. Therapy, which included confidence-building exercises and experiences, aimed to improve the boy's picture of himself as a worthwhile person, as one who could compete.

The twins were seen together for several sessions to observe more carefully the way they related to each other. The more passive boy almost invariably assumed that he would lose a game before it started, and superficially did not seem to be too disturbed about it. Yet, in the treatment activity program, the skills of the twins were fairly evenly distributed with one twin winning at one game and the other at another. Session discussions focused on this observation. The parents, who were both intelligent and sensitive people, continued to point out to the children their respective strengths, emphasizing that although they were different, each child had his share of assets. Both twins had the same basic intellectual capabilities, but the more aggressive, less "nervous" twin achieved at a more consistent and average rate, while the twin who felt inferior seemed to perform less adequately unless a great deal of pressure was applied along with confidence building. Then he achieved very well but began to show signs of increasing stress, so that the parents were advised to limit their concentration on academic achievement.

In talking with parents at Mother of Twins Club meetings, I found that many of them seem to feel that the need for professional advice reflects badly on them as parents. They may be perfectly willing to air their children's "adjustment" or "growing up" problems in public, but find a private consultation threatening because it implies to them that they have been failures. This is nonsense!

Mothers are generally more willing to seek professional help than are fathers, who seem to feel that to seek outside assistance is an admission of failure on their part. Many men have the idea that problems should be solvable within the confines of the family. Such solutions are no more likely to succeed than "do-it-yourself" medical treatments.

Just as you would note physical symptoms to bring to the attention of a doctor, you should also be sensitive to certain psychological danger signs. If they appear, discuss them with your family doctor, pediatrician, guidance counselor, school nurse, child psychologist, or child psychiatrist. Here is a list of things to watch for:

- A sudden or dramatic change in your child's personality
- An increase in fearfulness to the point where it interferes with day-to-day functioning or with sleep or other natural patterns
- Increased aggressiveness to the point where the child alienates other youngsters, siblings or parents
- Increased passivity or withdrawal from social interactions and more time spent in solo activities (Such children are often called loners and are sometimes overlooked because they seldom rock the boat; they may be involved in a fantasy world to the detriment involvement with the world of reality around them.)
- Socially delinquency by which the child gets into one batch of trouble after another
- Chronic underachievement and discouragement at school.

Most children who are brought to psychologists, psychiatrists or guidance centers have more than one complaint. Parents seldom bring in a child simply because she tells stories, or because she takes things, or because she wets the bed. It is far more usual for them to bring her in because she does all three.

Professional evaluation can help determine whether a child's difficulties stem from emotional problems, a learning disability, or being slower than average. A slow child in a normally moving classroom, for example, can become extremely frustrated and begin to act out in antisocial and attention-getting ways to relieve some of that frustration, and to gain some degree of stature and recognition in the face of constant failure. Or such a child may simply withdraw into a shell.

Children who learn new ways of behaving, so as to avoid alienating themselves and to enhance their skills in relating to others, will probably grow up to be much happier and well-adjusted people. Many who work with children find it so rewarding because children adapt more easily and more quickly than adults, and their patterns are not so deeply entrenched or reinforced.

There is nothing spooky, frightening or painful about a professional psychiatric or psychological evaluation or follow-up treatment (sometimes referred to as therapy, psychotherapy, counseling, guidance, etc.). Therapy can involve a variety of techniques, depending upon the therapist's training, experience or orientation. Studies have shown that it does not make too much difference what type of approach a therapist uses as long as he or she is well-trained and efficient.

Stages of Childhood

Whether we are dealing with a single child or twins, there is no doubt that the first six to eight months are the most difficult, particularly if this is a first pregnancy. How often parents remark that their worst mistakes seem to be made with the first child. And, of course, in the case of twins, if they are first, we make double errors! Without exception, all parents experience some anxiety and fear regarding the early development of their first babies, and those fears and anxieties sometimes have a way of affecting the way their babies develop. The firstborn are always watched very carefully, prodded, pushed and pulled, so they will develop "on schedule" or even ahead of schedule in order to measure up to some expert's standard, or to the neighbor's or relative's child of the same age.

Before I survey the developmental stages of childhood, I would urge parents to keep in mind constantly that while there are certain predictable developmental stages that all children go through, every child is an individual. Just because your child may be slow to reach a certain stage of development, don't jump to the conclusion that your child is retarded or impaired in some way. Likewise, if your child appears accelerated, don't be too eager to apply for admission to Harvard or Radcliffe!

What to expect from babies (birth to 6 months)
The human offspring is among the most helpless and dependent in the entire animal kingdom. Therefore, much of the earliest caring for human beings seems almost mechanical. Yet birth to 6 months can be a very trying time because of colic or other discomforts that result in interrupted sleep and irritability. Food allergies, too, until they are identified and dietary substitutions are made, can make life miserable for everyone. Nonetheless, small signs of growth serve to make it all worthwhile. How rewarding was that first genuine (non-gas-inspired) smile or laugh! What a good feeling comes from watching the infants respond to us by following us with their eyes and by "tuning in" to our voices.

The following are some high points of child development that pertain both to twins and singletons, along with some of my personal observations. (For more detailed treatments of developmental stages, see the Recommended Reading section at the end of the book.)

By 4 months, children no longer seem to be concerned merely with food and clean diapers. They become increasingly aware of the world around them. They are no longer content to lie in a crib on or in a playpen, but enjoy being held or propped up in a sitting position so that they can view the widening world around them. Photographs of our infant twins remind us how aware twins are of each other and how they attend to the movement of the other. Also, while lying in a crib, each baby can enjoy suspended mobiles, graspable objects, a variety of sounds and music.

By the sixth month, children are able to reach out into their environment, grab hold of things (like the other twin), manipulate objects and reach out their arms to be picked up. The children become increasingly mobile, scooting or crawling about, and as they advance toward the ninth month, with an increasing need for large motor activity, they may be ready for one of a variety of walkers or spring-type swing arrangements.

It is at this age, because of their ability to get around, that the babies seem to feel at least some degree of independence. Consequently, as they creep around exploring their environment, they frequently get themselves into some dangerous situations. Consequently, it is wise to remove "delicate art objects," which may accidentally be destroyed, from the path of the exploring infants.

Some may disagree, but at this age a child can be trained to avoid hazards. For example, if the 8-month-olds are scooting about on the floor and playing with electrical cords, television knobs or other potential dangers, mom and dad can tap their hands, with an accompanying "no-no," and then distract and redirect them into an activity which is not harmful. This type of training is ineffective if only the first step is undertaken, that is, if only the slap on the hand and the "no-no" take place. Invariably, they will return again and again to the nondesired activity until they can be redirected into an acceptable activity. For some reason, many parents have the distorted idea that, from a psychological standpoint, it is harmful to discipline children. This is far from the truth. Children need help to grow up to be sociable and acceptable human beings.

Children also need stimulation from an early age to maximize their chances for social, intellectual and emotional growth. This need can be fulfilled within the confines of the home, but both the twins and the parents will enjoy exploring a wider area of the world. Some parents find, however, that loading up the car with all the equipment needed to take care of two infants, whether for a day or a week or for a brief outing, is far from pleasurable. Until the children reach an age where they are more self-sufficient, many prefer to stay fairly close to home.

... from toddlers

As the infants approach the toddler stage, from 9 months to a year or later (sometimes as late as 17 or 18 months), they begin to explore actively, learning a great deal about their environment, and probably getting themselves into considerable trouble. It becomes increasingly necessary to set up situations where they can play relatively free from danger so that they are not interfering every moment with mother's activities.

At this age, we do not expect twins to interact in any truly meaningful way as far as play is concerned. If anything, their play can be described as "parallel" because, although they may be close to one another, their interactions are largely hit or miss, trial and error, and generally lacking in purposefulness. At this age, they do seem increasingly to entertain each other; because they are close together and doing different things, they mutually stimulate each other. Children at this age will generally lose interest rather rapidly in one form of activity or toy so that frequent changes are needed to prevent them from becoming bored, frustrated and irritable. They can be moved from one room to another, given different toys or household objects, intermittently placed in a swing or a walker, or even bathed.

Children in the 16- to 18-month range generally are highly impulsive critters, and want to do things now, finding it very difficult to wait, and they withstand little in the way of frustration.

... from 2-year-olds

The two year stage is notoriously difficult since at this time the children forsake a rather easy going, cooperative style, in which they are cute and constantly doing new things to please the parents and amuse each other, for increasing independence, which frequently takes the form of negativism. Hence many refer to this stage as the "terrible twos." With twins, that can mean a doubly terrible time, for the mother especially.

The 2- to 3-year-old child, from a temperamental standpoint, is not an easy child for other children, including siblings, to get along with. He or she is often very rigid and inflexible and extremely demanding, frequently showing mood swings, and varying between extremes such as "yes-no," "stay-go", and so on.

Your twins are now learning to assert themselves, learning that they can often get their own way or frustrate mother with one simple word ... "NO!" This may be the first time that mother and one or the other of the duo become involved in a power struggle, a clashing of the minds, which can lead mom to feel that she has a pair of "juvenile delinquents" on her hands.

If possible, of course it is preferable to avoid these power struggles. This may be easier said than done. If you make a request in the form of an angry demand, you and I know what the child's response will be ... probably an angry and definite "NO." Young children seem to be like little devices for picking up messages about the kinds of things that disturb, annoy, upset and otherwise frustrate us, storing the information in their memory banks, and then using it against us! They are also great imitators; if we are arbitrarily negative and say "no" to their demands, then they will likely follow suit. Two children the same age are likely to imitate each other's negativism, thus setting up a possible chain reaction.

Mothers of twins who have survived this stage know that the problems of independence and increased assertiveness not only affect each child's relationship to mother (which can be a full-time battle), but also demand considerable energy to supervise the assertiveness that goes on between the twins. It is not unusual for one to impulsively bite, hit, kick or otherwise attack the other when he cannot successfully grab a toy away for himself. This may well signal the beginning of an off-and-on, or as some parents report, a constant and lengthy competitive struggle.

Biting seems to be a particularly common technique for expressing frustration at this age. While some parents solve the problem by biting the child back, and while it has been reported to be effective in some cases, less risky procedures might include simplifying the play situation so that the child does not become frustrated so easily; supervising more closely; or trying to catch the child before she actually bites and quickly closing her mouth—a surprise technique which may soon make its point.

... from 3-year-olds

Three-year-olds seem to become somewhat smoother in their functioning, and characteristically the word "yes" begins to replace "no," to the pleasure of everyone in the family. Much of the earlier frustration has ebbed because the children have learned to speak. Their needs are more easily interpreted. They can do more things. Each now seems more interested in the other twin, other people and the world. Play is more complex, imitative, and cooperative.

Twins have been observed to engage for long periods of time in simplified role-playing games with each other or their other siblings. If they play house, for example, they might assign each other roles of father or mother, feeding, pottying, diapering, bathing or bedding dolls or stuffed animals. Often their movements are swift and Chaplin-like.

The twins may be eager to increase their social repertoire by becoming involved with other children their age. Their vocabulary increases and they become fascinated with new words. They can be taught to help themselves by partially dressing themselves and caring for some of their simple needs like getting a drink and washing their hands (after a fashion!). Often, twins show different needs for achievement in these tasks, with one far surpassing the other. Frequently, a more "retiring" or less independent child may enlist the aid of the other twin in such acts as putting on shoes, turning on the water, and so on.

Later in the 3-year-old stage, it is not unusual to observe stuttering which may be a reflection of increased incoordination in development. This incoordination may also be seen in increased awkwardness, falling, stumbling, tripping and occasional tremulous activity.

Exaggerated tension may be expressed in blinking, nose picking, nail biting, masturbatory activity or thumb sucking. Increasing demands for attention and reassurance show up as whining, crying or questions designed to assure the child of being loved.

... from 4-year-olds

Four-year-olds are expansive individuals, enthusiastic about new discoveries, exercising many new-found skills, throwing, hitting, and otherwise trying themselves out, sometimes at the expense of their twin. They may be particularly destructive at this age, and this destructiveness may be based on expansiveness or impulsiveness together with increased curiosity about objects in their environment.

This is the age, too, when many children develop a fantastic imagination; sometimes it is difficult for them to separate the real from the unreal. Many parents become upset because they feel that a child is lying or being purposefully misleading or untruthful. Here the principle of avoiding undue concern and alarm, so as not to inadvertently reinforce the problem, is an important one. Labeling a child as a liar at this age is dangerous because it has the tendency to prolong and complicate the situation.

This is also the age when children like to branch out. They are no longer content to stay confined in the backyard, and want to get out on tricycles and meet up with other youngsters in the neighborhood. This is the time in the child's life when it is sometimes very difficult for mother to begin "letting out a little rope." Children need to be taught the principles of safety in the form of "Don't go into the street." Such directives need to be followed up very consistently in order to determine whether or not a child can be trusted with increasing degrees of freedom.

Growing up should be a gradual process, with the parents letting the children have more rope or more freedom as they show some readiness to assume responsibility. If they handle one new freedom or responsibility well, then the addition of others can be considered. Many of the problems we have with teenagers result from holding back too long: our teenagers makes demands for freedom that go too far too quickly and they find themselves in a good deal of serious trouble.

... from 5-year-olds

Five-year-old children are moving towards increased independence and are more predictable than when they were 4. They tend to calm down somewhat and may be more stable and friendly. Some 5-year-olds may still be quite dependent on mother, particularly if they have not had the experience of nursery school separation two to three mornings a week.

Because they are "big" and going to school, they now need to do more things for themselves, and should be able to do much of their own dressing, except perhaps for tying their own shoes and more complicated tasks of this type. With twins, we may begin to notice, in a more pronounced fashion, that one is more independent than the other, more of a leader, more assertive, more dominant, etc. This is not at all uncommon, and it is nothing to become alarmed about. These dominant and passive roles may later change or may later become less obvious. For example, at the kindergarten stage, it is not unusual to find one twin in some ways helping the other to do more things without mother's assistance.

... from 6-year-olds

Six-year-old twins may present their parents with a very hectic year! They are increasingly more aware of the world around them; they have had nursery school experience and now kindergarten; and they may seem ready for the challenge of "regular" school. This is an age of increased experimentation, of trying themselves out, of trying new things, sometimes making excessive demands. Their increased emotional output may present a real challenge to parents, who may frequently find themselves wishing that the twins were at an earlier, more complacent and agreeable age. They may be exasperating because of quick, momentary changes from love to hate. Often, it will be impossible for mothers or fathers to determine just what has happened or what they could possibly have done to bring about these rapid changes.

In their quest for increased independence, children begin to assert themselves more by not wanting to follow directions as closely as before, by wanting to be their own person. Observations of 6-year-old twins indicate that this increased need for independence and experimentation as well as heightened emotionality often leads to more fighting and bickering between the children. School, particularly if they are in separate classes, can and often does provide the necessary diluting agent to keep them from becoming overly combative and competitive. Also, their interest in their own individual friends and peers becomes stronger.

The 6-year-olds' increasing sense of independence sometimes brings a resurgence of a type of negativism seen when the children were 2 to 2 1/2. Many different kinds of techniques can be employed in order to smooth out some of the difficulties that the children may be experiencing. Distraction, a great deal of support and encouragement, as well as displays of love and affection will help reassure the children that they are all right and still wanted and important to the family.

... from 7-year-olds

Seven-year-olds may be less exuberant, less bold, less outwardly friendly than they were; they may become more sensitive or easily hurt. They seem to have calmed down and in some ways may be easier to live with. They can become moody and withdrawn into more individualized kinds of activities. Also, they may prefer more passive kinds of entertainment, such as watching television or listening to the radio. They may spend a great deal of time with artistic endeavors, such as painting or coloring, or may involve themselves in individual kinds of play acting. They sometimes feel that they are victims, that they have no friends, and that they are being picked on constantly. They may feel that their family or school friends are being mean to them, and may have the desire to run away. There may even be physical complaints, such as stomachaches or headaches, and they may not want to go to school.

In this period increasing demands are being made of the children at school to work more independently, pay attention for longer periods of time, comprehend more and use more mature judgment. Likewise, at home, this is the age when most children start doing chores and experience increasing demands that the chores be carried out at a higher level. Also, they are beginning to feel that they are no longer the center of the universe, and they may not get as much positive feedback in the form of, "What a cute twin." They may be getting gangly, and sometimes even unattractive, and their concepts of themselves are beginning to change.

From now on the children gradually become more independent, developing their own friends and becoming more mobile, changing from a tricycle to a bike, and from walking and running in the near vicinity of the home to the broader scope of the neighborhood. This is the age when we need to encourage the twins to develop their individual friends, to visit them at their homes or to bring a friend home to visit. This more mature type of socialization is necessary for the children to develop their own styles in relating to others and to gain some feed-back from others as to what kinds of persons they are. From the mother's standpoint, probably more importantly and more practically, this branching out tends to dilute the rivalry and friction between twins, or twins and their siblings.

The primary school years are a time when we want to encourage the development of individual interests. To insist that both twins take piano lessons or guitar or dance may be doing them a disservice because it may add to the already strong competitiveness that may exist. If they take part in different activities, it is more difficult for them to compare themselves. Sometimes the children themselves may insist on taking the same type of lesson and in this case the competitiveness may be diluted by using different teachers, different dance styles, different piano techniques and so on. With boy/girl twins, we obviously don't have this type of problem to as severe a degree.

... from 8-year-olds

Eight-year-olds seem to be once again outgoing, experimental individuals with a good deal of enthusiasm. They are quick to respond and to enjoy new and challenging experiences; they often bite off more than they can chew. They may become unduly self-critical, however, and we may need to extend positive encouragement to keep them from feeling that they are failing.

... from 9-year-olds

Nine-year-olds often seem to abandon their parents in favor of friends and companions, and they find it difficult to limit themselves to the outside play hours prescribed by their parents. The children's desire to be with adults is likely to be limited to those kinds of activities that they themselves enjoy.

Sometimes children at this stage will develop neurotic symptoms. They may become more sensitive. They have stomachaches, headaches and vague physical complaints, which may be a forerunners to the physical changes that will take place in the pubertal period. They may use some of their neurotic complaints to avoid engaging themselves in responsible routines. They may be much more outgoing and negative, refusing loudly, putting you off when it comes to the demands that you might make of them. Sometimes 9-year-olds seem to be quite openly rebellious, and we wonder whether we have premature teenagers on our hands!

In the case of twins, it is possible to have two who are withdrawn, sullen and drag their feet, or two who are rebellious, outspoken and uncooperative, or one of each. In any case, I think that many of the characteristics one sees at any particular age may simply be a stage—that can be temporarily reassuring. If any of the troublesome characteristics persist for a prolonged period of time, a consultation with the family doctor, pediatrician, child guidance worker or child psychologist might be indicated in order to prevent some maladaptive behavior from becoming unduly fixed and permanent.

... from 10-year-olds

Ten-year-olds are often very enjoyable, especially as the children begin to behave in a very mature fashion, like young adults. If we are relaxed and friendly, they can frequently cooperate and, surprisingly enough, even make helpful suggestions or desire to help the family. This may also be the beginning of a deeper understanding and feeling, not only for each other but for the "kids at school." They may come home concerned about the way a child was maltreated or rejected by others. The feelings of empathy or "feeling with" someone else may be evolving, as well as the beginnings of tolerantly accepting others for what they are—a stage some of us never reach!

Preschool Issues

In this chapter we will look at some typical problems and concerns that confront the parents of young twins. First-time parents, especially, have plenty of questions about what is normal and what to worry about. More experienced parents may discover that they've fallen into a rut or some bad habits. All parents want the knowledge they will need to cope with the challenges that their growing children present.

Feeding
Many doctors do not like to allow infants to go home from the hospital until they regain the weight lost immediately following birth, or until they reach some specified weight, such as 5 pounds. Some newborn twins require frequent feeding, perhaps as often as every two hours, around the clock.

Mothers who before the birth had planned to nurse their twins may be overwhelmed when the time to do so actually arrives: the sheer impact of two hungry babies may frighten mothers—perhaps unnecessarily—from trying to breast-feed. Here the doctor and the lactation expert can be of assistance. They will be able to make recommendations on the basis of the mother's physical condition and limitations as well as the needs of the babies. The food value from prepared milk products or milk substitutes can be adjusted to fit the need of the individual baby. Some mothers find nursing twins too difficult; others have done it successfully and found it enjoyable. Some supplement breast-feedings with bottle feedings, while still others prefer to bottle feed exclusively. Bottle feeding may allow the mother more flexibility in her already very busy daily schedule. From a psychological standpoint, whether a mother nurses or bottle feeds may be less important than how she handles the feedings.

Today, with disposable bottles, diaper services, and disposable diapers, a mother's "busy work" is much less than in times past, so that, in this respect, she may feel that she has more time or freedom to nurse the twins—an experience that some mothers feel is extremely rewarding. There can be no real substitute for the closeness and emotional rapport that can be established in this way.

Psychological studies show that babies have a very definite need to be held, cuddled, spoken to, and responded to if they are to develop normally. Long periods of isolation in a crib with no stimulation from the mother or father can have a depressing effect on the growth and development of infants. Yet, if the infants are premature, some doctors have recommended that they not be held or fondled excessively, but that a period of "watchful neglect" be employed. In this case, your crib-side presence, talking, cooing, or singing to the children without excessive handling, would have some of the desired effect.

The feeding of two babies presents some problems, particularly in the middle of the night when the groggy parent is not sure whether she just fed Johnny two hours ago, or was it really Jane? For this reason, a tablet and a pencil with the recorded time of the feeding and the amount of milk consumed will help avoid confusion (and such a record would come in handy if the doctor should need this information). If the babies require several night feedings, the mother will definitely need the help of the father. Sometimes parents take turns with the feedings (if the babies are being bottle-fed) while at other times they seem to be able to "tune in" to the cry of one baby or the other. In such families, mother might retire early in the evening while father feeds and cares for the babies. Later, father retires and mother takes over the feedings. After father goes to work in the morning, mother may take a mid-morning nap (time and circumstances permitting!).

Feeding problems

Feeding problems with one child can be worrisome, frustrating and threatening enough for a young, first-time mother, but they can be downright terrifying with two! One or both of the twins may have food allergies that are only gradually discovered by trial and error. Colicky, irritable, crying babies who eat readily and then projectile-vomit can be a source of real concern. Caring for one or both twins with such problems creates additional stresses, lack of sleep, increased fatigue and irritability, and weakness on the mother's part.

Food problems can start very early in life and continue, or arise at nearly any time later. The two twins may differ tremendously in how much they feel like consuming. Some mothers become concerned if a child does not willingly devour three hefty meals a day. For some children, this just isn't in the cards. If the mother is overly nervous about food consumption, her anxiety might be picked up by these little receiving sets and used as a potent weapon against her in a continuing battle of the wills. Trying to feed infant or toddler twins together in nearby high chairs or other seating arrangements can result in chaos, hilarity, and/or frustration. At times, they seem to compete in dribbling, spitting, or in getting the food any place but where it should go. This type of mutual entertainment may have to be cut short by rearranged seating or separate feedings.

As they get older and develop more definite likes and dislikes we may find them exchanging unliked portions of food under the table. A relaxed attitude on the part of the mother and father at feeding time can eliminate many of the feeding problems that cause so much stress in some families. Excessive and rigid demands regarding how much and what kind of food should be eaten by each child may, in the long run, backfire. Dinnertime or any meal time should be as pleasant as possible; if dinnertime becomes a daily war, it might be better for the children and parents to eat separately.

Occasionally, differences between twins lead to bickering and competitiveness at meal time. Perhaps one cooperates and tries to please by eating everything, while the other balks, picks at the food and complains. Avoiding obvious comparisons, ignoring or distracting the poor eater may prove helpful. It is possible to use some competition without making unfavorable comparisons: "Who would like to try a new food tonight?" or "Are you ready to try something new?" In this way, we stress maturity and new opportunities to encourage them to try new foods. Going out to restaurants for dinner or to friends' homes for lunch, parties and dinners may be added incentives to break away from a fairly confined diet. Of course, if we introduce a wide variety of texture, colors and tastes in the infancy period, we will find it easier to continue to broaden and expand the children's taste as they mature.

Another technique to change the attitudes our twins have about food and meal time is to let them fix something else nutritious, if they refuse to eat what is placed before him. While this might seem to encourage noncooperation and stress individualized or "cafeteria" feeding, most rebellious eaters soon tire of the alternative, particularly if it's a peanut butter sandwich, and in time gladly resume a more well-balanced and varied menu. Along similar lines, allowing the children to serve themselves seems to promote the feeling that they have some control over what is happening to them and may avoid conflict of wills. Some observe that children who are allowed to help themselves may eat more and from a broader variety of foods in the long run than those who are not.

Bedtime

It is sometimes hard enough to get a single child to bed, let alone twins. All the elaborate methods used by single children for avoiding bed are well known to twins. They may become "Mr. or Miss Personality", the "Show Biz Kids," the endearing, lovable and talented offspring, when they are about to be banished to the bedroom and excluded from their audience.

Some mothers of twins, however, complain that bedtime is sheer torture. The strain of dealing with two live wires during the course of the day exhausts the mother and frequently leaves her with few emotional resources with which to deal with the cuteness and testing of two at bedtime. Father needs to lend a hand. Either he could deal with both children while the mother finishes up other responsibilities and has a breather, or each parent can handle one twin and so minimize the interfering interaction that usually takes place.

Ideally, there should be some type of ritual leading up to bedtime. Following dinner, the tempo, activity level or mutual stimulation of the twins should be diminished considerably. This part of the day should be a quieter period when children watch a quiet television program, engage in more sedate and passive types of play, or are read to. Outdoor play, except in summertime, should be discouraged. Roughhousing, wrestling and loud play should also be avoided. Violent television programs, jarring music and other forms of super-stimulation should definitely be taboo. Because the twins have likely been together for large portions of the day, they are likely to be irritable with each other and provoke each other.

Although bedtime should be at a set time so that the children can predict from one day to the next what will happen, it should be adjusted occasionally, earlier or later, depending on their hunger and fatigue levels and those of their parents.

The bedtime ritual could also include a bath or shower, which should have a soothing or quieting effect. With young twins, this experience may not be so quieting if they are bathed together, as they may continue to amuse, entertain and otherwise activate each other. Following the bath, the ritual continues with reminders to do all the usual things for which they will ask to get them out of bed later, such as using the bathroom and getting a drink of water. The ritual may include saying prayers, having a story, kissing and hugging and saying goodnight to the animals, making certain a favorite blanket or stuffed animal is handy, and so on.

After this inventory is checked, the children can be reminded that they are expected to go to sleep and that fun will continue tomorrow. If they chatter, laugh, fight or get out of bed parental visits with increasing degrees of firmness may be required. We should probably avoid further stimulating them by spanking, if possible, but their testing behavior needs to be consistently nipped. Sometimes, with younger twins, it may be necessary to separate them at bedtime by putting one of them in another room (they can be reunited again once they are both asleep).

If you allow one or both of the twins to get up and start entertaining, or if you cannot bring yourself to turn off the cuteness and cleverness, then all may be lost. Quietly and firmly march the children back to the bedroom as often as necessary. In most instances, however, a firm and consistent approach will pay off in the course of a few days to a week or two at the most, but in some instances clever and manipulating twins have been known to persevere to the point where locks had to be placed on separate doors!

Jerry Wyckoff, Ph.D., an associate professor of human development, suggested that, "During the preschool years, children often want to be close to someone when they sleep. They find it warm and comfortable to snuggle with another person. To deprive children of that experience is considered by some to be abusive. Children can, however, learn to sleep alone, and parents must decide whether the advantages of having preschool children in separate beds is worth the nightly war that generally accompanies separation at sleep times.

"Letting preschool children sleep together," Wyckoff continued, "has not been demonstrated to have any adverse long-term effects on children, nor has separation shown identifiable negative effects. Generally, children will tire of the hot, crowded sleeping arrangement and choose to separate themselves by the time they reach school age. If that doesn't happen automatically, it is usually easier to move a 5-year-old and keep a child of that age in his own bed than it is to try to contain a 2-year-old.

"If it is important to separate children," he concluded, "then they should be moved to separate rooms. Parents must be prepared to put children back in their own beds frequently because they often wake in the night and seek the comfort of someone else's bed. It seems much easier, however, to leave the sleeping arrangements up to the children at this age, and then deal with the problem later if the children don't resolve it on their own."

Nap time
Like bedtime, nap time, too, can become a battle. As one parent complains, "Our multiples are demons! They are in their 'twos' and they don't do anything without a huge fight, war or debate—especially at bedtime! We put them in separate bedrooms; and they are now sleeping better, fighting less, trading toys more easily and in time-out less often. But they still fight taking naps! How can I establish and keep a nap time ritual? All they do is work together to try and stay awake. Help—I need encouragement."

I definitely understand that the "twos" are sometimes terrible. As Jerry Wyckoff observes: "During the second year, children are learning to deal with limits or boundaries. Their reaction to these is to resist. As both children grow through the same developmental period, they also play off of each other and reinforce the resistance to boundaries imposed by the parents."

Wyckoff suggests that: "It is probably best to separate your twins for naps, just as you would for nighttime sleep." He would label this as a "rest time," and suggests that gates be placed in their doorways if the doors cannot be closed and fixed.

He also notes, "No research can be found to suggest that closed doors have an adverse effect on young children, in spite of the volume of noise they make when the door is closed. After a few days of their rest time ritual, the twins will probably take naps if they are tired. If they don't nap, they and you will at least get a rest period which you both deserve."

Night fears
Irrational night fears are not particularly uncommon. They sometimes are a result of children having been overstimulated, overly tired or frightened during the course of the day, or may be the result of some ill-defined anxiety which manages to focus on nighttime or darkness because of the separation from parents and the ensuing isolation. Some twins can arouse fears in each other; they can also assist each other to calm down. The best way to handle fears is to reassure the children that they are safe and that there is nothing present to harm them. A small night-light in the room or a hall light with the door left ajar may be all that is required. Many parents fall into the trap of lying down with the children until they fall asleep. What this action says is that there is something to be frightened of and that we are staying to protect them. Fears can sometimes occur during the middle of the night, and awaken a child from a sound sleep. In this case, one child may awaken the other; one or both may then proceed to get into bed with the parents. In this case, the children should be returned to bed as quickly and quietly as possible, reassured softly and distracted from the fear, and perhaps reminded about something pleasant that happened the day before or something that will happen the next day, then tucked in, kissed and told that everything will be all right. If the children are allowed to stay in your bed or if you return to one of their beds, you may be reinforcing and prolonging the fear.

Nightmares seem to be more common with boys, particularly those that are active or anxious or who come in contact with a variety of other children. Nightmares and night terrors seem to be a way that the unconscious mind has of revealing its worries and concerns and perhaps reliving in an exaggerated fashion something which happened the day before. In several pairs of identical twins, whom I have seen, night terrors seem to be more common in one child than the other, and may be related to his increased sensitivity and reactiveness to things that are happening in the family or in his environment in general. If there have been conflicts between the parents, unhappiness, illness, death or other frightening or unpredictable experiences, the overly sensitive child may not express his anxiety during the day, but may express it at night, when his defenses are lowered, in the form of a nightmare. Other youngsters become agitated and walk about in their sleep, but this does not always seem to reflect anxiety. They may simply be reenacting a scene from the previous day or acting out a fantasy.

Some nightmares in twins seem to be based on guilt over hostile feelings towards the other twin or even in death wishes. These may be considered extreme forms of competitiveness or rivalry in which their feelings are consciously unacceptable and thus the twin tends to "work out" the problem in sleep in the form of a nightmare.

Stimulation
Many of us, in our zeal to provide as much stimulation for our children as possible, often bite off more than our children can chew. How often have we taken the children out after a busy morning at home and gone to a new and different kind of place, such as a park, an airlines terminal, or a restaurant, and then followed this with another activity, only to discover—to our amazement!—that the children respond to our efforts by becoming whiney, tearful, agitated and generally miserable. We have to be able to gauge how much stimulation our children can take, and avoid reaching that point. When a child becomes overstimulated and irritable, he may sometimes find it impossible to settle down and take a nap or go to bed at the desirable time of night. We must remember, too, that twins are constantly stimulating each other and may not be able to take as much in the way of external stimulation as an individual child might. If there are single children in the family they, of course, further contribute to this stimulation.

TV
"My major objection to television is that it eats up children's time, is addictive and is not an activity," stated Janet Gonzalez-Mena, a child development instructor in a community college in Fairfield, California. "Instead of interacting with the world and each other, viewers are sitting passively and absorbing much that they probably do not need. But mostly, they are not learning to play with other children and get along.

"Most communities offer activity programs for 2-year-olds. This gives them a chance to learn to play with other children, to explore the world and to do the things that interest 2-year-olds. If you and your spouse do not agree on what your twins should be doing (watching or not watching television), this may make the issue even bigger than it otherwise would be, and the children can be picking up on this.

"Furthermore, if the children complain when you turn the television off, it is not a 'big deal'; 2-year-olds complain about everything!

They need to be moving about, crawling, climbing, walking and running, and engaging in gross motor activity. This is especially so if they are confined to the house in the wintertime."

I agree with Mena's assessment: children need to be directed into more active play. One of my strong preferences is to introduce more crude or "raw" materials such as empty cardboard boxes, rimmed cans, and smooth pieces of wood for building things. This not only requires physical activity, but also encourages creative imagination. These types of unstructured objects are probably more stimulating than highly structured, expensive toys that have a single purpose and require little imagination.

Toys

Questions frequently arise concerning what kinds of toys are best for young children. Often you don't have to worry about buying toys for the young twins as people frequently provide doubles, at least when the twins are young. Sharp-edged toys for infants are potentially dangerous, as twins can harm each other when playing close together. Look for toys made of plastic and nonpoisonous materials, toys that are soft with no protruding or dangerous sharp edges, suitable for children to learn to grasp hold of and place (as they undoubtedly will) in their mouths. Objects small enough to be swallowed should be avoided. (Plastic or rubber squeak-type toys sometimes have very sinister, small metal parts at the base which are responsible for the squeak, and can sometimes be chewed out and choked upon.)

Years ago some toys and baby furniture were painted with highly toxic lead-based paints that could result in brain damage to the child. It is very rare to find such objects today, unless they are of antique vintage.

Twins, even if they are boy/girl, often like identical toys the first year or two. Later, as we seek to develop individuality in the twins, we would not automatically buy them exactly the same toys, although it may become necessary from time to time.

A useful principle in the selection of toys for children is... Simplicity! Highly mechanized toys which run on batteries seem to be operable for very short periods of time, and do nothing but frustrate the child when they break down. These highly structured and mechanical devices leave little to the imagination of the child, and this is probably why they tire of them very quickly. An odd assortment of smoothly finished pieces of wood, scraps from a lumber company, is highly preferable to an expensive, highly elaborate toy with breakable moving parts.

The old-fashioned wooden orange or apple crate can be many different things for the child. Placed on its end it can be a refrigerator, a cupboard or a bookshelf; placed on its side it can be a stove, a desk or a counter; placed on its back it can be a sink, a tub or a boat. Children's rooms, family rooms and play areas should be functional and livable, and while children can be encouraged to pick up periodically and clean up their own messes, one should not strive to have a "Better Homes and Gardens" atmosphere at all times. An ample supply of raw material, such as old magazines, construction paper, string, cardboard, glue, crayons and paints can provide many hours of fun and good healthy experience during those times when it is not possible to go outside.

Creative Playthings® and Playskool® have lines of play equipment that are very durable and lend themselves to the development of creativity. There are funny, gimmicky toys that make children laugh; there are cuddly, companionable types of toys, like stuffed animals and dolls. Doll play for boys and girls is a healthy type of activity because it helps them to learn their respective roles as future parents. Identical twins or twins of the same sex may want to exchange roles occasionally and this is not harmful. However, it may be potentially harmful if a boy continues to prefer to play a feminine role or if the girl consistently prefers to play the male role.

One or both twins may become almost addicted to stuffed animals, dolls, various assortment of toys, blankets, etc. The parents sometimes ask whether this is dangerous and whether they should be removed. Children below school age frequently do have these kinds of habits, and we've all seen little Linus with his blanket dragging behind him. Some of these objects take on such importance that they seem to be extensions of the child's personality, or "self." In this respect, it could be potentially harmful to arbitrarily or suddenly remove the treasured object. My own feeling is that children will give up items on which they have become extremely dependent when they are ready to; you can perhaps accelerate this by offering them opportunities to decide whether or not they are ready.

Our own twins were conditioned to the soft baby blankets, and when they were tired or frustrated as toddlers, they would seek out the blankets. In time, the blankets became rather aged-looking and frazzled, and periodically frayed edges were trimmed so that eventually they got down to the size of handkerchiefs. One of them was accidentally left aboard an airplane and this did not result in any serious emotional upset to the child, but for months afterwards, every time he saw a plane fly overhead, he'd say, "There goes my blanket!" Subsequently, the other child was offered the opportunity to discard her blanket, which she eventually did.

Some toys and games are helpful in developing finer motor coordination in the hands as well as eye-hand coordination. These include the Playskool-type wooden puzzles which start out with one or two pieces and work up to more complex ones, such as maps of the United States. Coloring books, tracing books, clay, plastic or wooden letters of the alphabet and numbers are, of course, what we call educational toys, and sometimes have a very facilitating effect on the child's development.

One of the best forms of both entertainment and education is a chalkboard. It can be placed in the twins' room, in the family room or on the porch or patio. Use either the free-standing variety or the type that connects to the wall. Often the chalkboard becomes the focal point for other kinds of role playing, including playing school. Twins can exchange roles as teacher and pupil. It is amazing how much they actually teach each other; an older child, of course, can teach younger twins new things before they're introduced to them at school.

Toys often lose their interest after a while. Rather than leaving the large assortment of them out all the time, you can put some of them away and bring others out. Alternating toys in this way is like having Christmas several times a year.

Children will use toys more often if they are kept where they can be seen and reached easily. For example, it is much better to display toys on wall shelves than to have them in a toy box in which the toys on the bottom are seldom seen. The shelving does not have to be expensive; it can consist of a series of alternate bricks and boards or the inexpensive hanging variety.

Outdoor toys and games

Twins need opportunities to develop large muscle skills, such as those involved in chasing each other, climbing, riding tricycles and bicycles, swimming, skating, sledding, skiing, etc. Obviously, none of us lives in a climate that would permit all of these activities all year round, so we have to make do. An outdoor swing set is a great way for them to release a large amount of energy and to get some healthy exercise. Fortunately, with two children, they are likely to be satisfied to stay at it longer because of the "company factor." Climbing bars or pull-up bars are also effective. Tether balls and punching bags are great objects for the release of pent-up anger and energy in overly active boys and girls.

A large packing crate can be at one time a house, a store, a fort, a jail, and anything else the youngsters want to create. Outdoor recreational equipment does not have to be expensive, but there should be enough in the way of opportunities to encourage them to stay home at least part of the time and to attract their friends.

Destructiveness with toys
Obviously, two children are going to be harder on a toy than one. The life expectancy of a boy's toy may be shorter than that of a girl's, although this is not always the case. Normal wear and tear is different, though, from destruction. Unfortunately, no one single approach will handle all destructiveness. The first question one asks is, Why does the child break toys? There are many different reasons:
- The children may fight over the toys and in the struggle break it.
- The toys themselves may be of the "instant destruct" variety—cheap plastic designed to last about fifteen minutes.
- An overly busy, hyperactive, or high strung child will often break thing because of an impulsive tendency to act before thinking and the fact that such a child just covers more territory in the course of the day than a typical child. With these kinds of children, prevention is generally the best approach. That is, don't let this type of child have toys, gadgets or equipment that are likely to be broken. A child who has broken something carelessly should be told very clearly that this is unacceptable behavior; usually some type of dramatic and repeated effort on the part of the parents is needed to drive the point home.
- Some children inadvertently or accidentally damage things out of curiosity—"What makes it work?"—and as we all know it is easier to take something apart than it is to put it back together. These experimenters can be discouraged from taking on tasks beyond their years by substituting objects that are appropriate for them to experiment with at their age level.
- One of the most common "toy destroyers" is the angry, hostile or aggressive child. In a fit of temper, an angry child may even tear apart one of his own prized possessions. Pointing out the self-defeating quality of this kind of act may be the best punishment, and the fact that the child no longer has that object, of course, is a punishment. But meeting the child's aggression and anger with your own anger simply adds to the child's already high level of aggression, rather than dissipating it or limiting it.

Fighting, sharing, biting
Since 3-year-olds are generally in the process of separating from their mothers as well as from each other, there is bound to be much sorting out of what is "me" and "mine," according to Eileen Pearlman, Ph.D. (Dr. Pearlman is a psychotherapist, the director of TwInsight and a frequent contributor to TWINS® Magazine. She is herself an identical twin and is married to a fraternal twin.) As they develop a greater sense of self, they will want more independence, while still at times needing to be dependent. It may be unrealistic to expect that

they will consistently get along and not fight. Fighting and competition occur in any twin relationship, even the healthiest. A certain amount of bickering and arguing is a rudimentary form of problem-solving; and if a parent attempts to prohibit this, it might do more harm than good.

Parents can sometimes reinforce bickering by paying too much attention to it; telling children to go off and bicker in the other room may also prove unrewarding. Pearlman suggests that using a timer when twins are sharing a particular toy might help to neutralize the situation. Even toddlers can be taught to set the timer themselves and assume more responsibility for the sharing experience.

Sharing is an important social skill, but you needn't insist that each child share everything. It will alleviate some bickering if you can duplicate some of the particularly prized toys, whenever possible.

One common fighting tactic used by young twins is biting. When their children bite, says family and child psychologist Jerry Wyckoff, Ph.D., parents should use the opportunity to work on frustration tolerance and problem-solving, with children being rewarded and praised for playing together successfully.

For example, saying, "You are getting along so nicely," "I like the way you're getting along," and "Thank you for getting along" are ways to reinforce good behavior, while time-out can be used for inappropriate behavior.

Rules should be clear and logical: "You may play with any toy that's on the floor, shelf or in the toy box, but if someone has it in hand, you must wait until it is put down."

When a child's ability to play within the set boundaries breaks down, as it undoubtedly will from time to time, you should help out. Problem-solving involves holding the child who is frustrated and talking through options that may be available. Say, for example, "Let's see if we can think of other things to do instead of crying, biting or throwing a tantrum."

Language

During the second year language becomes a greater part of the child's total behavior. Though vocabulary can develop very rapidly, it is important at this time to use simple commands and short statements to be sure the children understand. For parents to continue using "baby talk" is uneconomical because it means the child must learn two words instead of one. Although it may be cute, it does not lead to a smooth, forward moving maturity. One should not insist on the correct pronunciation of all words, but by giving clearly pronounced examples when introducing new objects such as "toy" or "dog" or "milk," parents give the children a clear model to copy. It would be better to allow a child the privilege of saying "mik" for "milk," rather than encouraging something really far out, like "moo moo."

Stuttering

Speech development continues at a very rapid pace; sometimes stuttering becomes a problem now, though it may occur at any age. At this age, it is related to the child's inability to say things as quickly as his mind thinks them. It is usually short-lived, and the best method for correcting it is to avoid making much of it: by all means avoid labeling it as "stuttering." It seems that with stuttering, as with many other childhood problems, making a fuss over the action, or labeling it, serves only to reinforce it. In some more extreme cases, a pattern becomes established as part of the child's image of himself, as though he says to himself, "I am Johnny; I am a stutterer."

Twin lingo

Identical twins show striking similarities in pitch, tone and other qualitative features of their voices. Nancy Segal, Ph.D., director of Twin Studies at California State University, Fullerton, reports that in studies of identical twins reared apart, conducted by Susan Farber, 20 of 21 pairs were found to be similar in tone and pitch. Furthermore, the majority were either "talkative" or "taciturn" in their manner of speaking.

Many investigators have also commented on the similarities between twins' laughs. In one study, a pair of identical twins reared apart came to be known as the "giggle twins" as they not only laughed frequently and in the same way, but almost exclusively in the presence of the other twin! A number of more recent studies of twins' language development and disabilities also reveal greater resemblance between identical twins than between fraternal twins, consistent with the genetic influence on these traits.

Some identical twins, as language is or should be evolving, begin to develop their own unique language patterns, which only they can understand. While this sometimes appears to be cute, in the long run it has the effect of limiting the child's communication and shutting out others in the family. It can also interfere with acceptance by peers in a nursery school, kindergarten and sometimes 1st grade. These unique language patterns should be discouraged, perhaps by more separations of the twins, either through diluting their play times by introducing other youngsters, or by using nursery school placement.

Children who are slow to talk, or who have no speech at all by the age 3, should by all means be enrolled in a nursery school program. One of the frequent reasons why they do not speak is that nearly all their daily needs are anticipated and met without their having to express themselves verbally. Outside the home, however, and in an organized group, a child's wants are not that easily anticipated, and the need to speak will be much more acute than at home. Thus, I frequently advise a period of preschool experience before making a referral to a speech therapist.

Toilet training
I feel that too often we rush our children into toilet training before they are ready to succeed at it. You have probably heard a proud mother state that her child was toilet trained at 6 months, or some other early age. Most of us would agree that, even if she is speaking the truth, it is the mother who is trained at those ages and not the child.

The push for toilet training in the case of twins is certainly understandable, and I am in complete sympathy with any mother who desires to "dry up" the children so that she doesn't have to spend so much money on disposable diapers or time washing cloth diapers or even just collecting them for the diaper service. However, psychoanalysts feel that the danger of toilet training too soon results in some long-range personality problems. They feel that an individual so trained can become overly meticulous, too compulsive, too fastidious about cleanliness in general. At the other extreme are those permissive souls who are perfectly content to allow their child to wet up a storm well into his third year.

In general, I think we have to employ the principle of readiness. It would, therefore, be a good idea to start placing the child on a potty seat at about 18 months, either at the same times each day or at different times, depending upon what ensues in the bathroom! If after diligently and consistently trying this pottying procedure for a week or so, no significant habit seems to be forming, abandon the procedure for a month or two, and then try it again.

Potty training is a complex physiological process involving relaxation and release of the appropriate musculature at the right moment, and between pottyings it requires an awareness of body functioning and enough control to avoid mistakes. Toilet training procedures should begin as pleasantly as possible. By avoiding drudgery, punishment or pain in the experience, we will increase the chances for more rapid success. I have found that having special toys in the bathroom area, which the child can only use at that particular time, serves to divert attention and make it easier to follow through with the desired activity. In the case of our fraternal twins, the girl became fascinated with mother's old compact, and the boy put pennies in a piggy bank. They were successfully trained in a period of only a few days at the age of two after brief and unsuccessful attempts at 18 and 20 months.

The quality of the relationship between the mother, the father and the children is important in toilet training. If the child wants to please the parents by doing something new and mature, and if the parents give a great deal of praise for successful efforts and avoid too much punishment for unsuccessful ones, the procedure will probably be far less painful for everyone involved.

Children who have persistent problems controlling their bladders may find the social pressures of a preschool class sufficiently motivating to clear up the wet pants rather rapidly.

Thumb sucking
One of the most frequent complaints that comes to the attention of the pediatrician or other child specialist is thumb sucking. I am not convinced that it is more common in twins; others, however, feel that because twins are together from such an early age, they may mimic each other in this as in other ways. Thumb sucking day and night is not unusual up to about 4 or 4 1/2. After that age, it generally decreases in frequency and tends to be associated with sleeping. It is a carry-over from the early "oral period," when the child learned that discomfort could be eased by sucking a nipple. Sucking movements are one of the few inherited natural instincts, and some children begin sucking their thumbs even before birth. In any case, the association of the thumb with feeling fulfilled, feeling comfortable and gratified are built up over time, making a very strong habit. And we all know that such habits are difficult to break. Many of us have other oral habits that are difficult to break, including smoking, drinking, and chewing gum.

Unfortunately, there are no simple, do-it-yourself rules that always remedy this kind of problem. Thumb sucking may be an attempt to console oneself in the face of frustration, fatigue, boredom, or a feeling of emptiness. Thus, we have to ask ourselves, as the child gets older, to what extent he is really happy and feeling a part of things.

Like many other childhood problems, probably the less attention paid to it, the better. Parental harping, or criticism from brothers and sisters, simply adds to the frustration and may increase the need for self-gratification or self-pacification. Thumb sucking will often stop as a result of the child's growing up or maturing. Involvement in a nursery school program may fulfill some of the need for stimulation, and we find a decrease of thumb sucking in this period. Also, the child may be embarrassed to suck her thumb at nursery school.

There are a few children who persist in sucking thumbs past the usual cut-off point of kindergarten or 1st grade. As a matter of fact, I know of a 16-year-old girl who still sucks her thumb at limited times, such as when she is waiting for her date to arrive! Certainly, thumb sucking past the 2nd grade level can mean something more than simply a resistant habit pattern. Some parents of twins, both fraternal and identical, report one twin thumb sucking much longer, and on close questioning it generally would appear that this twin has other problems as well. For example, one mother noted that one of her identical girl twins sucked her thumb in the fourth grade and that she also has feelings of being unloved and unwanted. In this case, as in many others, the thumb sucking was simply an outward symptom of something more serious brewing beneath the surface, which needed to be investigated and talked about with the child.

Many different techniques are tried with varying degrees of success:
- ignoring the problem
- removing the thumb when the child is asleep
- icky-tasting medicine
- verbal threats
- rewards or bribes for stopping
- physical punishment
- embarrassment.

Most therapists feel that when children are ready to stop they will—that is, when their needs are met, when they are comfortable within themselves and the family, and when they have outgrown the wish to suck. Frightening a child out of a habit like thumb sucking too often results merely in a substitution—like hair pulling or twisting, or nail biting.

Preschool

Preschool for 3- to 4-year-old children has much to recommend it. Unless there are other youngsters in your immediate neighborhood who are the same age as your twins, the children's experiences are likely to be quite narrow, limited, and unorganized. Also, a preschool with qualified and trained teachers is by no means a mere baby-sitting agency or a hit-and-miss arrangement. Preschool teachers are trained to deal with the kinds of growth problems associated with that age. Learning to get along with other youngsters at this age can be of great importance. Associating with other children has the added advantage of preventing your twins from becoming unduly dependent on each other, or at the other extreme, from becoming unduly irritated and hostile with each other.

In some communities, preschools are licensed, making it easier for you to choose an appropriate placement. In many communities, however, preschools are not licensed, and it is sometimes difficult to differentiate them from the type of establishment in which "old Mrs.

Jones" on the corner may be baby-sitting twenty children in her garage. In this case, it is necessary for the mother to make inquiries and determine whether the teachers are formally qualified and competent.

Preschools today appear to have another very important role to play. Since the advent of the first sputnik, our educational system has undertaken some significant changes. For example, in many communities today, kindergarten is no longer strictly playtime or just a socialization experience. It is a time when children are taught the beginnings of reading and numerical skills, and are exposed to much by way of organized field trips. Therefore, children are more sophisticated by the time they reach 1st grade than they have ever been before.

Thus, the preschool period is truly important in helping children increase their attention span, learn to sit still, and learn some of the necessary rudiments of conformity, as well as new kinds of free expression. They should also learn how to get along with others in groups, cope with rules, and how to give, take and share, so that they are emotionally and socially prepared for kindergarten.

Readiness for school
Because of the tremendous individual differences among youngsters of preschool and kindergarten age, we must not set rigid time tables for when the children should begin either their kindergarten or 1st grade experiences. The principle of "readiness" is an important one and has a significant bearing on when children are able to do what we (sometimes arbitrarily) expect of them.

For example, when children are ready to talk, when their nervous systems are sufficiently mature, and when they have the need to express themselves, they will talk. When ready, they will very likely settle down, pay attention and not be easily distracted (other things being equal). Some children, because of general or specific types of immaturity or developmental delays, will not be ready to progress to the next stage, either from preschool to kindergarten, or kindergarten to 1st grade, at the usual times.

Sometimes it happens that one twin progresses faster than the other and is ready to advance while the other is not. This need not be a tragedy. This situation will be easier for you, the parent, if you keep in mind the fact that they are individuals and not an inseparable unit, and if you adhere to the principle of meeting each twin's needs.

We often feel that to be kept back or retained is the worst possible thing that could happen to the child's ego. But, if the child is supported and encouraged, my own feeling is, if in doubt, hold the child back. So many learning problems that occur later on in the academic experience seem related to a child having to cope with complicated learning principles before being ready, from a maturity standpoint. It is interesting to observe that, in some countries (Scandinavian countries, in particular), reading skills are not taught until the child is 8, because they recognize that individual differences exist and that some children cannot grasp the concepts or deal with the symbols that are necessary in reading.

School-Age Issues

To separate or not to separate

Many of the questions asked by parents of twins have to do with the advisability or inadvisability of separating twins in school. In order to answer these kinds of questions, one has to realize that there are many different situations involved here. Identical twins, who tend to be more dependent on one another, should probably be weaned from each other gradually from a early age as suggested in the previous chapter. If the twins are occasionally separated prior to the start of school, so that one twin has an opportunity to be apart from the other twin on weekends or even briefly during the week, then they are not likely to become overdependent on each other.

While it is perfectly acceptable to have twins in the same preschool program, it becomes more desirable to separate twins at the kindergarten level, encouraging them to develop their own individual friends and to elaborate their own personality styles. Most schools, as a matter of course, recommend that twins be separated. Keeping them in the same classroom encourages overdependence on each other or increases the tendency towards competitiveness which is already, as we all know, enough of a problem.

If the twins are in the same room, the teacher may be too conscious of what they can and can't do as compared with each other. Greater allowance should be made for individual differences and different maturity rates. One mother of kindergarten twins writes: "Susan attended the same class as her identical twin sister Sandra. The teacher's only comment on one report card was, 'Susan is more aggressive than Sandra.' On the other, 'Sandra is less aggressive than Susan.' I know who's more aggressive. I wanted to know how they relate to their peers. The teacher seemed preoccupied with their twinship and enjoyed comparing one to the other. She did note one other thing that discouraged me from placing them in the same class in the 1st grade. Susan tended to answer questions addressed to Sandra because of Sandra's shyness."

Separating identical twins in the primary grades is probably beneficial when it allows the child to feel more unique, more individual, and assists in developing an individual identity. Far too often, twins become too dependent on each other. They are used to playing together at home, so if they are placed in the same classroom, they may not reach out for other playmates. Parents of children who are a year or so apart but end up in the same grade are very reluctant to allow them to be placed in the same classroom because of possible rivalry and the lack of opportunity for each to develop a unique style of independence. The same concerns apply to twins.

However, our boy/girl twins, announced at the end of 4th grade that they would like to try being in the same room for the 5th grade. They felt that they were mature enough not to become involved in childish tattling or to interfere with each other's right to independent activity. Rather reluctantly, my wife and I discussed the matter; because of their enthusiasm, we finally agreed to consider it. There were certainly some advantages: one of them had the bright idea that they could help each other with their homework! After some direct and indirect questioning, to determine whether there were any unhealthy or hidden motives for their desire, we agreed, and a request was made to the school that they be allowed enroll in the same class.

Things went relatively smoothly, and there were no crises. There was little or no tattling. They seldom shared the same friends (it was still the girls against the boys and vice versa!). Report card times were uneventful because we had already set the pattern, "Your report card is your business, and we (your parents) will be happy to discuss it with you privately." This approach was necessary because each child had particular strengths and weaknesses, and it was not realistic to expect that they would both do equally as well in all subjects. Consequently, there was no more of a flap about grades than there had been in the past.

I thought it might be interesting to get the twins' impressions about the experience. I had them each make a self-evaluation. Tracie wrote: "You feel sorry for your brother if he gets into trouble. If your teacher gives you homework, and your brother does it at school, you get mad at him when you bring home lots of homework and he is outside playing. You feel dumb if your teacher says girls talk too much." And Scott: "Well, first, when your teacher asks your sister a question and she doesn't know, you do feel embarrassed for her. When a kid comes up to your sister and teases her, you really get bugged, plus I have to tell him to knock it off or else ... It seems you love your sister at school but not at home. Plus, kids tease you about the way she acts sometimes. I think, just once, a kid should have his twin in the same class to know what they're like."

We did have to deal with the speed with which the boy did his work, as opposed to the girl, who was more deliberate and cautious—again individual differences are a fact, though we tried not to place a particular value on one or the other. The boy's observations that being in the same room allowed him to see what his sister was "really" like at school, and that he sympathized with her and felt compelled to defend her were interesting as well as encouraging. We didn't always see this at home!

It is very difficult to make any hard and fast rules regarding school placement; but my impression has been, from this and other experiences, that separating twins in the early primary grades does allow the children to develop their own academic as well as interpersonal skills. These are very important formative years, and we should do anything we can to promote healthy development.

I had the opportunity to discuss this issue with a disturbed identical 20-year-old male twin recently. He stated that he did not like being always in the same class with his brother because other youngsters tended to treat them as though they were the same person. Needless to say, this was very confusing to the twins. Eleven-year-old identical twin boys also have told me that they respond both to their own name and to the name of their twin because they are so easily confused in the same classroom and on the playground. If the twins' desire to be in the same classroom is based on a genuine feeling of comradeship and of wanting to assist one another or to enjoy the same experiences, it may be all right; but if the desire is based more on a neurotic dependency, then it may be harmful. Sometimes it will be difficult for the parents themselves to tell what motivates the twins' desires, and some professional assistance may be needed.

With fraternal twins of the same or different sex, there is generally not the same novelty as with identical twins, and they are seldom mistaken for the same individual, so that, if they do end up in the same classroom, the effects are generally not as bad. Fraternal twins who do not desire to be in the same classroom often express the fear that the other twin will tattle if they misbehave in school, or feel that there is enough togetherness at home and that this does not have to be extended into the classroom.

What if one needs to be held back?
Retention of a single child may be a heartache for parents, but the possibility of retaining one of a matched set always seems like a tragedy, particularly after the 3rd-grade level. However, if we have already set the precedent for treating the twins as individuals, then this need not become a hideous dilemma. We must also remember the importance of considering what best meets each individual's needs. Many school policies, principals' decisions and teachers' inclinations lean toward not holding a child back, because of a fear of emotional repercussion. This is why it is so very important to assess accurately a child's readiness for kindergarten or 1st grade. If you have the strong feeling that one twin lacks the maturity for the step from preschool to kindergarten, or from home to kindergarten, or from kindergarten to 1st grade, you should probably follow it; generally your suspicions will be well-founded because you know your child better than anyone else. Unfortunately, it is sometimes difficult to convince the teacher of this.

For a twin who struggles and experiences consistent failure, presenting a possible retention as an opportunity to catch up, a chance to avoid harder work or lots of homework so that there can be more time for fun next year, may make it easier to swallow. Making supportive, positive statements about the child's abilities and strengths should help. It is much easier for a child in kindergarten or first grade to repeat than for an older child because circle of friends is very narrow and because retention in kindergarten or 1st grade is so common. It is probably not wise to have the child repeat with the same teacher, although sometimes this is impossible to avoid.

Because twins have grown up together and have been so deeply involved with each other, the feeling of failure that the one twin may experience as a result of having to repeat may require additional steps. For example, in extreme cases, when a child who must repeat feels grossly embarrassed and absolutely cannot face his peers, it may be wise to transfer the child to another school within the same district. Also, if family finances permit, the slower child or more immature child may be able to avoid repeating by attending a private school with a smaller number of children per class; with additional, special attention, he might be able to catch up. A tutor is sometimes helpful in avoiding repeating, as is summer school.

Homework
Homework conjures up all kinds of negative feelings in most children because they have already been confined in school all day and have had to comply and conform with multiple demands. Only the highly disciplined and achievement-oriented child enjoys or tolerates well schoolwork that has to be done at home and at a time when most children want to relax, play and have a change of pace. Nagging children about doing it usually produces more negative feeling about the task. Looking over their shoulders or becoming too demanding and nosy (as the children see it) will only add to the frustration.

We as parents should be interested and concerned about our children's homework without being oppressive, dictatorial and demanding. For example, making inquiries about what a child is learning in Social Studies, casually looking over a textbook or papers that have been brought home, showing some enthusiasm in making a contribution or a comment about that topic, may take the edge off the negative feeling.

Many children do not have the staying ability to be able to go into their bedroom, or wherever they study, and follow through in a goal-directed fashion to the task's completion. Nor, perhaps, should they be expected to do so. Many tasks appear voluminous, gigantic and impossible, and it is up to the parent to reduce the task to more bite-sized pieces that children can handle—something that they should later learn to do on their own.

For example, one of our twins came home one evening very frustrated at the thought of having to practice his multiplication tables. He sized up the requirement as an impossible task, looking at it as a memory task involving 1s through 10s. With the aid of some multiplication flash cards, the task was reduced to taking the 2s and 3s one night, 4s and 5s the next, and so forth.

We added some fun, challenge and humor to the learning process in the following way: We went into his room and we used the chalk board to go over the tables a few at a time. We played a game in which I, initially, was the teacher and asked him the answers to the questions. Then we switched roles and he became the teacher and I was "Little Slow Poke" in the front row trying to remember the tables. He also got to keep all the flash cards that he had learned in rapid order. The more difficult ones we rehearsed again, and on succeeding nights, until he had completely mastered them. When he had all of the flash cards in his pile, his reward was a baseball mitt, something he needed anyway for Little League.

Some people consider this bribery, and I don't recommend using this technique with all homework assignments, but in this particular instance the combination of a fun learning experience with some humor and a reward was effective, resulting in the rapid acquisition of a large amount of learning material.

Sometimes parents feel that too much homework is being assigned, so that children themselves have to stay up too late at night and do not having any time for themselves. In this case, the teacher should be consulted to find out what is going on. It may be that a child is not doing as much as he or she should in class, and so has too much left over to do at home. This may be due to a behavior problem, a learning difficulty or general slowness. Whatever the cause, it should be identified and remedied.

At some PTA meetings, I have heard parents complain that there is not enough homework. Many parents feel that children get by too easily, that the primary years are important for establishing good study habits that will be necessary later, in high school and at college. My own feeling is that children should be encouraged to complete at home tasks that they have not been able to finish in school and that homework should gradually be assigned to children at about the 3rd- to 4th-grade level.

The reason that many teachers do not administer homework is that they have serious doubts as to who really does the work. Most parents make very bad tutors because we lack patience when working with our children over homework. This is understandable because many of the approaches to teaching are different today, what with modern math and more advanced teaching technology. Also, the role of a parent is a complex one. It involves many demands and "teaching" may not be one of the skills that a parent possesses.

A child who falls behind in an area of schoolwork should be encouraged to discuss the matter with the teacher. More individual attention may be needed to find the trouble spot.

And then, there is always the child who says all the work has been done at school, who has no homework to do, but who, at the end of the first 9-week grading period, receives unsatisfactory marks because of failure to follow through on assignments. It is unfortunate that so many weeks have passed before the parents realize how far behind the child is. In such cases, I have suggested that during the subsequent grading period the child take an index card to school, on which the teacher or teachers note every Friday whether assignments are up-to-date. This type of close supervision and observation seems to help many children assume more responsibility; they may not be ready or sufficiently mature to do it on their own.

Grades

Even when twins are placed in different classrooms, there may still be a tendency to compete for grades. I have always felt that grade cards are private, that they are meant to be discussed between the child and the parents, not among the siblings. They should not be used to engender or arouse increased competitiveness between twins. If one of them feels badly about not achieving as well in a subject as did the other, we have to ask ourselves whether the child is capable of better, and if so how can we go about helping the child achieve at a higher level. (Here a conference with the teacher seems important.) The child may simply be less gifted or even limited in some area; individual differences must be spelled out in order that the less successful child can compensate for feelings of inadequacy. In any event, the child should be encouraged and verbally rewarded in those areas of excellence, as well as in those areas where there have been difficulties and there has been improvement. Far too often we parents focus on the one or two poor grades that the child has, fussing about these while ignoring strengths in other areas. Interested and concerned parents should pay attention to the weaker areas and provide assistance, without making the child a failure and a disappointment to them. If a child is having difficulty early in school, parents should maintain close contact with the teacher and/or the principal. Sometimes an obvious personality conflict can occur, in which case the child should be changed to another classroom.

Morning problems
Chaos before school is a frequently reported occurrence in many families. This is more likely to be a problem where there are twins or more than one child. Complaints range from the slow, dawdling, daydreaming child who needs constant prodding—at whom mother finds herself yelling from one room to another to remind him of the quickly passing time and the approaching school bus—to the busy, active child who gets up two hours before everyone else and has gotten into a variety of situations, not always productive.

Conflicts sometimes arise when one twin is a fast starter in the morning and agitates the slower twin. Sometimes both twins may be slow or fast. When fighting, bickering and mutually irritating behaviors result in unpleasant, unhappy and unappetizing early morning hours, we need to think about prevention.

Usually, the best time to deal with these crises is not in the midst of them or immediately following them. If mother or father speaks quietly to the twins prior to bedtime, when (one hopes) things are somewhat quieter and more settled, the message may be much more effective: "Things were pretty unhappy around here this morning, and we seem to be yelling at each other. How do you think we can make things happier tomorrow morning?" By making the children part of that problem-solving situation, we can lead him to feel more responsible for changing their behavior the next day. For the slow-moving child we might suggest an earlier arising time, give periodic calm reminders as to the time, and encourage as much preparation the night before as possible, such as laying out clothing, completing assignments and having things ready for school.

The early risers who get themselves into trouble need to know when they may leave their bedroom and in what quiet activities they may engage so as not to wake up others. You could perhaps assign them some chores, such as feeding a pet, bringing in the milk, straightening up their room, making beds, etc. This would provide them with goal-directed and productive activities. If they can't or won't stick to activities that you feel are appropriate, then set more severe limits. For example, they may have to remain longer in their rooms with strict supervision for a few mornings to make sure that they learn to stay where they should, until they are willing to follow a more cooperative plan.

If the twins annoy each other in the morning, periodic *calm* parental intervention may be necessary to facilitate a smoother functioning household. Keeping a sense of humor in the face of these kinds of problems is not easy, but our attitudes are easily picked up and mimicked by the children.

I remember hearing a celebrity mom explain that she found it enjoyable and rewarding to have fun with the children in the morning, to laugh and joke with them (she was a professional comedienne) and send them off to school in a good mood. This seemed to lay the ground work for better learning and a better attitude about school as well as a better feeling about home. She felt that anyone could learn to make a bed or to carry out responsibilities at any time in life. Ten years from now the fun the family shared together and the good, happy feeling they had about school would be much more important than hashing out unimportant details. We need not overlook responsibility or the training that goes along with chores, but perhaps sometimes we emphasize training and responsibility at the wrong time.

Chores

Frequently, one twin is more cooperative in doing chores than the other. Apparently, from an early age, this twin has learned that one way to please the parents and gain a good deal of recognition and reward is to cooperate. The other may feel it is useless to compete in this area and so behaves the opposite way.

If one thinks of a family unit as a small piece of democracy in action, then it follows that each family member contributes something to the unit as well as getting something in return.

We have all observed that very young children often want to help with a project well beyond their maturity and ability level. The 4-year-old wants to help mow the lawn, the 5-year-old wants to assist in nailing back the shingles on the roof, and the 6-year-old wants to help paint the bedroom. In developing in our children a healthy attitude toward helping out, it is a mistake to say arbitrarily, "No, you can't do that, you're too young!" The child becomes angry or disinterested, and runs off to other amusements. When our children offer or volunteer to assist us in an activity which we feel is beyond their years, we should substitute a simpler task and give him positive praise for their assistance. For example, young twins can hand dad nails and pull weeds, or help mom put groceries away, and clean out the car.

Working together on family projects is a very good way of demonstrating cooperative efforts and may assist twins in becoming more mutually helpful and less oppositional. Far too often we expect them to happily do those chores which we ourselves don't want to do! For example, almost without exception, every boy in America seems to be required to take out the garbage. This does not mean that he should not take out the garbage. It does mean that sometimes we stereotype our children's roles according to their sex in such a way as to deprive them from becoming well-rounded and capable of handling a wider variety of responsibility.

The early encouragement of cooperation among twins in putting away the toys (for example), regardless of who used them last, may set the stage for continued assistance. Demonstrating that two can do the job faster than one by actually timing them individually and then together can further demonstrate the positive aspects of working together. You have heard one twin say, "If you help me, I'll help you," which makes chores less unpleasant and at times they may even enjoy themselves.

Children do not like to feel like servants in their own home any more than we like to feel that way. They might feel better about doing things for us and for themselves if we observed, "I need your help" or "Would you help me to ... ?" Many parents become angry and frustrated when a demand, such as, "Go do the breakfast dishes," is not carried through immediately and with a cooperative air. Yet, how many parents make requests of each other that are not carried out immediately? Here is another example of how we, as parents, provide the models after which our children pattern their own attitudes and feelings about doing things. If we as husbands and wives, or mothers and fathers, feel good about doing things for each other and comment about it, our twins will be more likely to enjoy the rewards of pleasing each other. If our marriages are unhappy and we make unreasonable or angry demands of each other, they are likely to mimic this, too.

A father of boy twins may get much more mileage out of them in the yard by saying something like, "Let's go work in the yard together," or "I need your help in the yard," rather than, "Go mow the lawn." Frequently, fathers of boy twins make very bad comparisons as to which one is more helpful, productive and independent.

There are many approaches to planning which chores the twins do. Here, it depends on the age and sex of the twins as well as how much legitimately needs to be done by the children. In those families where both mother and father work, there is obviously a greater need for the children to learn to do more for themselves earlier.

Sometimes they are sufficiently mature and cooperative to be able to take very direct recommendations as to what they will do. Other, more independent children will insist that they do not need directions, but can do it alone. Others bristle at certain chores and see them as unthinkable, undesirable or unacceptable. In this case, a rotating assignment of chores may be the best measure. Sometimes it is not realistic to expect that children will remember voluntarily to do all those things which they are supposed to do and, in this case, a check list or daily reminder may avoid a great deal of bickering or nagging on the part of parents. Informal family conferences to iron out inequities and job assignments may be helpful.

Sometimes we wait too long to start assigning or changing duties. There is no reason, for example, why primary school–aged twins cannot be taught to make their beds. One obviously does not expect that it will turn out to look like something a licensed practical nurse might have done in the hospital, but, by the same token, verbal praise will oftentimes provide them with enough of an incentive to want to do more to please their parents.

With twins, it may be a mistake to introduce competitiveness in the form of "let's see who can do it best," because one of the pair may decide not to participate in the contest!

Sometimes, boy/girl twins will become embroiled in arguments over the equity or inequity of chore assignments, with both seeing their jobs as more complex, more time consuming, more difficult than those of the other. If one is doing a variety of outdoor chores that take a lot of time and sees the other doing indoor tasks that seem insignificant, nonproductive or less time-consuming, or visa versa; it may be enough to let the first know how valuable his or her assistance has been.

Twin allowances

I believe that allowances should be given irrespective of chores so that the children have spending money for expenses like school lunches or to buy small items that they want. The amount of the allowance thus depends on the number of such needs and the family budget. It is thus conceivable that one twin may require less of an allowance because of the opportunity to earn spending money while the other has fewer opportunities for "independent income."

It is important for the twins to have some money for their own use and to learn how to deal with it efficiently. Children who do not have a small amount of spending money may be tempted to take it from others, from parents, from siblings, or from friends at school. One of the first questions I ask when a parent complains of a child's stealing is, Does the child have an allowance?

In my opinion, children should receive a "bonus," added to the basic allowance, as a reward for work above and beyond the call of duty. I think in this way the twins learn to connect expenditure of effort with monetary reward. Thus, a more industrious twin will have a chance to work toward some desired goal faster when willing to exert himself more. Each twin may be more motivated motivated to earn extra money at some times more than another. This policy also avoids undue rivalry and arguments if individual preference and individual motivation are stressed. This kind of competitiveness between twins is not all bad. If a child has to work for something, it may be more meaningful.

The twins may ask for expensive items that are either inappropriate for them to have, or beyond the scope of the family's income level. Their willingness to work and save for such things is a good test of how ready they are to have them or how badly they want them. For example, I know a 10-year-old male fraternal twin who wanted a mini-bike because some of his friends had them. His parent thought this was an inappropriate request because there wasn't enough space to use it and because this child lacked the necessary maturity and good judgment; nonetheless, they told him that he could have one if he could save enough of his own money to buy it himself. After a considerable amount of figuring, he announced to his father that realistically it would be a while before he could afford to buy one. This approach gives a good deal of responsibility to the child and avoids considerable family conflict.

Identical twins, or fraternal twins of the same sex, are more likely to desire two of the same expensive item. For example, 12-year-old girls both want their own stereo, a problem in this particular family because of limited finances. Fortunately, the girls were highly motivated to work around the neighborhood at odd jobs and saved their money over several months. In the end, they compromised, buying one unit and spending whatever was left on records. They decided that they could cooperate now and buy another stereo and more records later.

However, in the case of 10-year-old identical boys who both wanted expensive 10-speed bikes, such a compromise was not possible. Nonetheless, they pooled their efforts, jointly did yard work and other neighborhood work, and with some parental investment were able to wheel off to school on their own bikes.

Allowances, bonuses, work at home and extra jobs in the neighborhood make it possible for the children to make a very important investment in their own belongings. They are therefore likely to treat these objects with respect and perhaps develop a sense of responsibility for their care and upkeep. (This training continues if they are also required to pay for repairs!)

Birthdays and presents
When twins are young, it is usually convenient and fun for them to celebrate their birthday together. As they grow older, however, and develop their own circle of friends, it may become more cumbersome, particularly if the twins are boy/girl (or fraternal) and have different interests. There does not seem to be anything particularly sacred about birthdays, and no harm comes from allowing the twins to hold their parties on different days. Many nontwins do anyway because of the interference of school, conflicting activities, or inconvenience. For a number of years, our twins held their birthday cele-

brations on different days, taking turns being first. Occasionally, they would decide to celebrate together in order to have an ice skating party, a swimming party or some such activity. We encouraged them, for obvious practical reasons, to keep the number of children invited to between six and eight.

Sometimes there are questions or problems which arise in the minds of the twins' friends or the friends' parents as to whether to purchase identical gifts. The twins' friends are probably tuned in to the individual characteristics and interests of the twins and will probably make good suggestions to their parents as to what each twin would like.

At what age do you let them go to parties alone? What is the common etiquette? Sometimes parents of a child who wants to ask one of the twins to a birthday party don't know whether or not to ask both. Boy/girl twins, particularly when in different classes, are often not identified as twins. Because individuality and independence are such important considerations for twins, I think their friends should be encouraged to invite the one they want to invite. If the other twin's feelings are hurt by not being asked, a parent or friend could do something special, singling the child out for a special occasion, independent of the other twin. A pair of 10-year-old boy/girl twins I interviewed recently understood this point; both agreed that they were glad their mom let just the invited one attend. "We are not connected at the hip," said one. "We have to learn to stand alone."

Bickering and fighting

Bickering and fighting between twins can sometimes be merely a loud form of problem solving! At other times, it is pointless and endless and, to say the least, very annoying. Quarrels will be more frequent if one of the twins is especially irritable. Likewise, if one twin has a thinner skin, is more sensitive, more defensive and less secure, the ground work is well laid for a good deal of noise. So often we parents enter into the squabble without really knowing how the thing started or what it's all about. We end up taking a very arbitrary position, directly or indirectly siding with one to the chagrin of the other.

It may be useful—after tempers have cooled—to talk about arguments, pointing out the futility of most of them and exploring alternate ways of solving conflicts. You might, for example, set up a pretend situation in which conflict is likely and then prompt the twins find a way to solve the problem without coming to blows or screaming at each other. This sounds very idealistic, I know. I'm sure there are times when you would rather fling this book at both of them than sit down and try to be so rational. Yet, the exercise may be as valuable for us as for the twins.

If our twins fight and bicker, and argue and scream, we must ask ourselves from whom did they learn this? Generally, and even naturally, there is some arguing between parents. Children, as little receiving sets, pick up these techniques very early on, and it is sometimes embarrassing to see ourselves acted out in our children's fights. We may need to learn new ways of solving problems between ourselves so that our children will learn more productive methods.

Parents have rights and privileges in their families, one of which is the right to some peace and quiet. If this peace and quiet is constantly interrupted by fighting, then let the children know how it makes you feel, and suggest that they do their fighting out of your earshot. Simply stopping the fight and saying, "Please go outside into your bedroom to finish your battle," may bring it to a quick halt.

When the children have become embroiled in an arguments over something that concerns the whole family, such as the choice of where to go on an outing or at what restaurant to eat, rather than our make an arbitrary decision that would appear to favor one of the children, I prefer to isolate the children and set them the task of solving the problem among themselves in whatever way they can short of murdering each other. Surprisingly enough, this frequently works.

When there is fighting during a family game or activity, I have stopped the activity and sent the fighting participants out of the game and into a problem-solving situation out of ear-shot. Once, I was surprised to find the twins returning five minutes later arm-in-arm congenially talking to each other. They were allowed to reenter the game, and we all enjoyed ourselves much more. Later, I overheard one of the twins saying to his mother, "Dad always falls for that love stuff." Be that as it may, the important thing to me was the fighting had stopped, the conflict was resolved and harmony was restored.

Stealing

Stealing is one of the most frequent complaints that parents list when they bring a child in for consultation. Children who take things that do not belong to them arouse parental ire, are embarrassing, and sometimes arouse fears of long-term delinquency.

Stealing is a descriptive term often poorly and inappropriately used. In my experience, it seems more common for one twin to "take" than for both. Labeling the "taker" as a thief, or the behavior as "stealing," may affect the child's concept of himself negatively, and lead to feeling of being the "bad" twin. If we label children as "stealers" and reinforce this enough, they begin to think of themselves as thieves and act accordingly. This is a characteristic that we don't want inadvertently to foist upon our children.

Why do children steal? I am sure that there are almost as many reasons as who do it. There do seem, however, to be several clusters or groups of reasons why children take things. Regardless of the reason, I feel that it is very important, at least initially, to avoid referring to the child's taking of things as "stealing." The word "stealing" has such strongly negative social connotations that it may cause additional difficulties.

Some reasons for stealing:
- Some children take things from their twin brothers, sisters, parents, neighbors, friends or the store because they simply do not have the means to get what they want otherwise. In other words, they do not have money. Young children who want something take it. They need to learn that there are certain acceptable ways of going about getting what they want, and they also have to learn that they cannot always have what they want when they want it. An allowance goes a long way toward preventing children from taking things.
- Sometimes children take things because they feel insecure. We have all heard of the sort of character who surrounds himself with worldly goods to make himself feel better about himself. In the same way, there are children who take things out of the feeling of insecurity or inadequacy, usually in relation to a rivalrous situation with a twin or a brother or sister. The things that such children take are not really things that they need at all. Mothers sometimes say that they find all kinds of useless "hardware" piled under a bed, in a drawer, in a corner of a closet or in another secret hiding place.
- Other children take things in order to be benefactors among their friends. These, again, are the type who feel inadequate about themselves, but instead of hoarding their treasures, they hand them out freely, as if they were the last of the big time spenders! This type of child is in effect "buying friends." This is the boy or the girl who, if asked for a piece of gum, will gladly give an entire package, or will find some excuse to give money or other treasures to a potential friend in order to feel assured of a place in the group.
- And then there are children who take things because they are angry at their parents or at others, taking out of a conscious or an unconscious need to get even. Such retaliation generally results in embarrassing the parents. These are the children who take money from the pocket or the purse of a close friend or relative or even a neighbor. Naturally, the discovery of the loss and the tracing of the "theft" arouses very strong feelings on the part of the parents.

Lying

"Lying" is another poorly used label that may reinforce or prolong the very behavior we are anxious to eliminate. Again, this kind of behavior is more apt to be seen in one twin than in both. It may well be part of the "bad" twin's repertoire.

Many parents overreact to a twin's tendency to exaggerate, spin yarns, and otherwise embellish what's going on in life. A youngster from four to six years sometimes finds it difficult to draw the line between imagination or fantasy and the real world.

We do not want to squelch or cut off imaginative thought completely because much of it can be creative. In the form of play or role-playing, it can be self-amusing and productive.

Many times a father or mother tells me, "I can't stand a liar!" Honesty is seen as a primary virtue, and a child who lacks it is assumed to have no virtue at all. Yet, studies show that when you come right down to it honesty is a relative thing. How many of us adults "lie" to ourselves in the course of a day or a week or a month or a year?

If one twin is storying or distorting reality, or in other ways not telling it as it is, then we have to ask ourselves, Why? Here are some possible reasons:

- The child cannot yet accurately tell the difference between the real and the unreal, and this may simply mean a lack of maturation.
- If it is an exaggerated thing, and this has gone on well beyond the six-year level, it can sometimes be the sign of a defect in of "reality testing". In other words, some children honestly cannot tell when they are being dishonest.
- Sometimes one twin lies to get the other in trouble.
- We occasionally put our children in such a position that it is literally impossible for them to be honest with us. We zoom in on them as though we were FBI agents or prosecuting attorneys preparing for a real inquisition. In such cases, the children may try the odds to see if they can "get away with it."
- Occasionally, children will distort reality, exaggerate or lie because of a need to appear more adequate and better in the eyes of their parents. These are the twins who feel inadequate or uncertain about their position in the family, and who feel the need to enhance their concepts of themselves in the eyes of their parents, which they try to do by exaggerating.
- Another type of exaggeration is story telling. A mother once told me how her father was baby-sitting with the twins and one of them greatly enjoyed listening to him spin exaggerated yarns about his own childhood. Because this was such a rewarding and

entertaining experience, he learned to do it himself in order to amuse his friends and attract attention.
- Very closely related to the story teller is the twin who out of a sense of inadequacy exaggerates or lies to gain attention and approval. One must ask the question, Is there something wrong in my relationship with the child that prompts the child to exaggerate?
- Lying is often seen as one among many symptoms in emotionally upset children. For example, children coping with divorce and remarriage of the their parents or other distressed family situations commonly show a combination of lying and stealing.

In foster homes and sometimes in adopted twins older than 3 or 4, these symptoms can be interpreted psychologically as "testing" techniques. The children are asking, "How much do you really love me? How much do you really want me? How much will you put up with?" In these instances, the children have to be told in whatever way they will understand that they are wanted, that they are loved and important family members, but that we will not put up with some of their testing behavior.

Testing can be seen in children other than those adopted or in foster homes. Children use many maladaptive behaviors to see just exactly where their limits are, and how firm the parents will be in maintaining those limits. Testing out these limits seems to be a constant process, and the more consistently and firmly we hold the line, the more we add to their feeling of security.

Sex interest and sex education

Children, being naturally curious, and twins, being reared close together, soon become aware of their own bodies and the body of their twin. If they are of the same sex, curiosity about the body may not come about as soon as if they are of different sexes.

Bathing infant twins and young preschool twins together in the tub solves many problems, and there is nothing wrong with it. We do not want to develop a sense of shame or unnecessary modesty in our children. When they ask questions about their sexual apparatus, we need to answer their questions at the level they can understand. Putting off sex education until they are preteens or teens is unrealistic because they will find out much earlier. It is much better to feed them information gradually regarding the "mysteries" of sex than to allow them to develop their own frequently distorted concepts.

Many parents wonder whether children should be allowed to view adult bodies. This largely depends on how the parents feel about it. If the parents are self-conscious, uncomfortable or anxious, the child be, too. Some authorities feel that exposure of the adult naked body to a child of the opposite sex after about the age of 5 or 6 leads to complications in the relationship, and produces unnecessary sexual stimulation or curiosity for the child.

We need to be sensitive and alert to the questions the twins ask. Sometimes they have discussed their puzzlement together before making inquiries of the parents. Sometimes they are not sure how to ask about what is bothering or confusing them. They may not ask questions at the most opportune time. One twin may use the other as the spokesman if he is too embarrassed to ask himself. We should be sensitive enough to recognize what our children are really asking. "Where did I come from?" may not relate to reproduction, but geography. Preparing ourselves to answer their questions at their own level of sophistication is a must.

Fraternal boy/girl twins may not discuss sex openly or share their newly discovered information. However, boy/boy and girl/girl twins are more likely to giggle privately, whisper and otherwise secretly share sexually provocative stories, jokes, new words, signs or expressions, signaling that they are ready for some sex education. Clarification of the "words" or translating them into acceptable language will generally reduce the "gutter talk" considerably.

Twins, regardless of whether they are identical or of different sexes, will be curious about each other's sexual parts, more than about other parts because they are generally covered with clothing. The normal amount of supervision will prevent undue preoccupation with sexual concerns early in their lives. Leaving them alone for long periods of time and with little supervision can sometimes result in mother discovering them playing "doctor" at a very tender age.

How we deal with this kind of sexual curiosity and experimentation is of great importance psychologically. If the mother and father are mature and sexually well adjusted, they will be more apt to treat the matter firmly and unemotionally. If they become unduly alarmed and emotionally distraught, the children may develop some very mixed feelings about sexual development, and these guilt feelings can later interfere with their own progress toward sexual maturity.

Sex play and masturbation
Twins are sometimes noted to experiment or mutually stimulate each other sexually at relatively early ages.

How should parents handle the twins when they have been discovered in sex play or masturbation? Undoubtedly, the response will depend upon the parents' attitude about these matters. If the parent responds with shock, horror, disgust, fear, or other strong negative feeling, this will probably only complicate things. However, at the other extreme, permissiveness, approval or encouragement does not seem to be the answer either. A more moderate approach would be to ask the question, Why are they doing what they are doing? Is there something missing in the children's lives? Is there some reason they turn to themselves for gratification and pleasure rather than turning to their parents? Are the children's emotional needs being met? Are they sufficiently stimulated, loved, accepted? Are there conflicts you are aware of that interfere with the relationship between the twins themselves? Occasionally, a habit is formed simply because the child experiments with his own or mutually with his twin's sexual parts, finds it pleasurable, so he does it again. In any case, these questions should provide us with food for thought in attempting to understand their behavior.

With preschoolers, distractions and closer supervision may be all that is required. If children begin to stimulate themselves in grade school, and it becomes apparent to the teacher and/or the parent, a firmer approach may be needed. In effect, they are performing an act that is both socially unacceptable and a signal of an underlying emotional problem.

Preteen and Teenage Twins

Ongoing relationship building
As twins approach and enter the teenage period, many parents become frightened and threatened by the prospect of not being "in control." It is as though the size of the children constitutes a decided threat, often felt by both parents. Some parents get into difficulty by becoming embroiled in arbitrary power struggles with their children. Where twins are involved, these struggles will most assuredly meet with defeat because of the twins will tend to stand together in the face of the challenge by authority. Points of conflict or disagreement should therefore be dealt with outside of a power struggle ("Yes, you will," "No, I won't"). Major wars may be averted if the conflict can be resolved through discussion, airing of feelings by both sides, and solutions brought about through compromise and experimentation with new ways of doing things.

Because parents will periodically need to intervene and impose limits on preteen and teen behavior, they must continue building their relationships with their children. If the parents and twins have opportunities to grow together, to know, understand, respect, accept and tolerate one another (which is a tall order!), then those times when disciplinary action are taken will not seriously jeopardize the relationship and cause serious breaches within the family.

A fraternal teenage twin recently remarked about how difficult her teenage years were because, as she said, "Not only are my sister and I having problems, what with our own moods, but so is mother. This makes for a rotten time at home." She was referring to the fact that she and her twin were experiencing some of the emotional growing pains of puberty, while at the same time, to compound the difficulties, mother was undergoing menopause. This, then, is surely one of those instances when professional assistance is needed to cut down on the conflict and to facilitate relationships.

Influence of the peer group
We all hope that our twins will ease into adolescence smoothly and go through this period of change without great turmoil. If their emotional needs have been met—love, acceptance, respect and continuing understanding—there need not be any serious problems originating from within the family. We all recognize the strong influence of the peer group and its ability to swing teenagers away from family influence. As the twins mature and become more independent, they may, understandably, not want to participate routinely in family outings with younger brothers and sisters. The need to be accepted by a group is as great with twins as it is with singletons. But by

no means should we abandon family activities; these should be retained if possible.

Also, because of the importance of gender identification, mothers and their girl twins and fathers and their boy twins should continue to enjoy their respective activities and relationships. If father and his twin boys enjoy sharing common interests and participating in some of the same activities, then their chances of continuing communication with each other are far better. If the twins do not share the same interests, the parents may not be able to participate equally in the activities of both, but they can spend time discussing and encouraging each twin's interests.

As the twins' peer group takes on added value and importance for them, parents may see their influence with the twins diminishing and find their offers to spend time with them rejected. Just remember that it is necessary for the twins to be accepted by their peers and to have fun with others, outside the family. Twins may not affiliate with the same peer group. One twin may prefer to go his own way, and avoid as much social contact as possible with the other twin. After all, this is the period during which both twins will be working toward the desired goal of establishing independent personalities and lives. Continuing to encourage the twins to develop individually in this area, as well as others, will avoid the overdependency that can be observed even in some teenage twins.

Who am I? Which one am I?
If one had to choose a single concept to reflect the major concern of most teenagers, it would have to be that of identity or self-concept. In other words, they are asking questions such as, Who am I? What am I? What is my role? How am I different from my twin? What will I eventually be? Adolescence, that strange period between youth and adulthood, is a metamorphosis in which there can be a great deal of anxiety and concern. This worry may focus not only on the physical changes, which are obvious, but also on the mental changes that are experienced privately.

Outward signs of change
Identical twins grow and develop similarly, with occasional slight variation. Fraternal twins of the same sex can develop at very different rates. Some girls resent their rapid, early development. Because they appear to themselves awkward, they often stoop or use poor posture to deny their height in relation to their shorter male peers. Fast-growing girls should be encouraged by their mother and prepared to expect various physical changes prior to their onset, to reduce surprise, anxiety and resentment against growing up.

Differing growth rates for fraternal girls can be a problem for one or both, but the important guiding principle remains the same: Stress the individual differences. Generous reassurance for the troubled twin will help her in settling down to accept her rate of growth as nature planned it—something to which she can and will adjust. A rapid growth rate is generally not as traumatic for identical twins because they have each other for consolation and mutual support. Delayed or slow maturity for girls can also produce worry and anxiety.

Given a choice, boys would generally prefer an early, fast growth spurt, as it has a potent meaning regarding their maleness. Boys are likely to compare themselves and their bodies as opportunities present themselves in physical education classes. Failure for one twin to grow and develop secondary sexual characteristics as quickly as his twin may lead to serious feelings of inadequacy or inferiority. Small 13- and 14-year-old boys sometimes become obsessively preoccupied with their size. Worrying, withdrawing, daydreaming, they can make themselves miserable. Their grades may suffer, and their gloominess and despair can affect the entire family. Some cope with this stress by "overcompensating." They may become belligerent or even develop a temporary, or on occasion, a permanent "small man syndrome."

Outward signs of changes sometimes bring complications because they may appear more awkward, angular and physically unattractive than they have thus far in their lives. Yet, when performing specific athletic skills, or dancing, or driving, they may be very coordinated and capable, and should be reminded of this to help them see the fuller reality of their predicament.

How teenage twins feel about themselves is to some extent determined by what they see in the mirror. The unique kinds of physical problems they find may or may not be under their control.

Inner problems

The inner problems of teenage twins are related to how they feel about themselves as unique and maturing individuals. How they develop this self-concept depends to some extent on how they see each other. The kind of feedback they get and the cues they receive from their families, peer groups, teachers, and virtually all those people with whom they come in contact are a definite influence.

For twins, the change from a child's to an adult's self-concept can be complicated by the fact that two of them have grown up together and have similar mutual positive experiences. The situation can be even more complex in the case of twins who are competitive, or when one has taken on the concept of the "good" and the other, the "bad," or one, the "superior," and the other, the "inferior."

When twins are able to meet each other's needs, to complement each other and to assist and support each other in their struggle for independence, this can be one of the most enjoyable periods of their lives. It can be a time for either being together in common activities (even double dating) or being apart through involvement with different groups, without pangs of separation anxiety. It can mean encouragement and reassurance when one is low. It can also mean the sharing of special moments during those happy times.

The situation, however, is not always so pleasant. A mother of 14-year-old identical twins asked, "What do you do when the nastier twin takes advantage of the other?" Here is an instance of the continuing "bad vs. good" dichotomy or polarity, where one continues to get attention by conforming and doing acceptable things with the family and the other undoubtedly gains attention by aggravating other family members and in nonconformity. Here are two individuals, born at the same time, of the same family and raised in the same circumstances in which one nonetheless feels very differently about himself. The classic vicious cycle is set up in which one twin does something unacceptable, is responded to with negative treatment, feels badly about it, and does something "bad" again to get even, and so the cycle is repeated. The same kind of conditioning exists in twin teens where one feels adequate, competent, secure and confident, while the other feels inadequate, lacks confidence, and feels stupid, unliked and unloved. It is as though one selects positive and rewarding kinds of feedback from those around her, while the other distorts the type of feedback she gets, and feels drastically different.

Sometimes, an accident, an injury or an illness severely cripples or impairs one twin, which has a decidedly negative effect on his or her self-concept. It is hard enough for a singleton to learn to overcome the devastating feelings that accompany such a trauma. The feelings of having once been whole, healthy and normal, and now being permanently impaired, and inferior, and looking and feeling differently, can have far-reaching and at times catastrophic effects on personality structure and development.

For example, take the case of identical twin boys who had the normal amount of competitiveness, had healthy self-concepts, and were well-rounded academically, socially, athletically and musically. One was involved in an automobile accident that caused permanent brain damage which resulted in lowered intelligence, shortened attention span, loss of some memory function, and impaired physical coordination on one side. His frustration would be bad enough if he had been a singleton, but in a family where he had a mirror image twin—that constituted an ever-present reminder of what he might have been. It took several years of psychotherapy to help him reconstruct more realistic goals and a new identity, quite different from those of his preaccident self. He was encouraged to take up different kinds of activities so as to avoid comparing himself unfavorably with his twin.

"Who am I?" Many times, teenage twins have difficulty in identifying their own unique qualities and separating them from those of their twin. Sometimes one complains of not knowing where she stops and her twin begins. At other times, one may be confused by what he sees as dual or multiple personalities within himself. Feelings of highs and lows and both socially acceptable and socially unacceptable ideas may generate fear. They ask the question, Which one of all these people am I really? And they need to be reassured that all of us are made up of many different parts; all of us play many different roles at different times in relation with different people.

If the twins are adopted or foster children, they often begin to ask very penetrating questions about their natural parents and may feel the need to know why they were "rejected" by them and what kind of people they were. This happens even in those families where adoption has been discussed frankly and openly from early childhood. Sometimes they attempt to find the natural parents in their quest for self-definition and identity. Nevertheless, because of the amount of time, devotion, and emotional investment that has gone both ways between the twins and the adoptive parents over the years, they can look to these parents as guides in constructing their self-concepts.

Promoting responsibility
"Neither of my girls has any sense of responsibility or respect for their own or others' property. I feel that this is definitely my fault, but is it too late to instill the right values at this age?" asks a frustrated mother of 11-year-old identical twin girls. It is probably not too late. Generally, twins and singletons do not automatically become "monsters" as they reach that magic age of 13. Growing up and maturing is a gradual, step-by-step process.

Ideally, as the twins do more things for themselves and for the family, they will in turn gain more opportunities for additional degrees of freedom. In this way, they continue to grow towards independence, which is the ultimate aim for all of our children. We need to let them know very definitely what is expected of them. If they are able to carry out their responsibilities, then they have demonstrated that they are mature enough to earn the opportunity for a new privilege. One of the most valued privileges is some type of group or peer activity. Whether or not they are allowed to continue to have this privilege depends upon how they conduct themselves.

In some families where twins have been overly indulged, and where no realistic expectations were made of them earlier in life, one cannot expect mature behavior automatically at the onset of the teenage period. In one case, 13-year-old fraternal girl twins complained bitterly because they were now expected to earn their own spending money. Their frustration was natural. Why should they be expected to do housework now? Why should they suddenly be expected to behave in a highly independent fashion, when they were encouraged to be dependent all their lives? This particular pair took an almost sadistic pleasure in watching their parents squirm. This was one of those families in which the parents, because of the many sacrifices they had to make while growing up, wanted to provide well for their own family. Many well-meaning parents forget that hard work is a character-building and maturing experience. In those families where everything is provided, where all needs are met instantly, and where the children do not have to make sacrifices, the children may well suffer from a lack of character.

Independence
One of our main goals as parents in raising our children is to prepare them for eventual independence. Yet, many of us become very frightened, threatened and angry with our teenagers when they start showing the normal need for independence. This need can reveal itself in many different ways. The twins may become increasingly argumentative and quarrelsome with each other, with their mother, father or other siblings; they may become disrespectful, or increasingly irritable and sullen. The fact that they disagree with us need not be a threat to our position as authorities. If we develop relaxed attitudes about their disagreements, allowing them to discuss them openly or to "blow off a little steam," this may clear the air and relax the relationship. We need to avoid becoming overly defensive in our reactions to these discussions.

Teenagers commonly experience an inner conflict between independence and dependence. This can be seen when they demand more freedom one moment, on the basis of their increased maturity and age, and then very soon after give some expression of marked dependency on the parent or the other twin.

Sometimes the need for independence is reflected in either camouflaged or very open and overt rebelliousness. Some forms of rebellion may actually assist in the development of a feeling of self-confidence and emancipation. We should help our twins by directing them towards those types of activities that offer healthy, honest avenues for the expression of feeling and that at the same time accomplish some good.

Sometimes one twin is more emotionally and socially mature, and is capable of handling increasing responsibility and freedom earlier than the other. The less mature one may become indignant because if not allowed the same opportunities as the sibling. Sometimes, it is difficult to help this twin see that physical age in and of itself is not the only deciding factor as to when one is or is not allowed to do something. Here again, parents should stress that, although they are twins, they are also individuals and will therefore be treated uniquely.

With fraternal boy/girl twins, there can be conflicts centering around the "double standard." That is, parents may allow the boy more freedom earlier than they do the girl, believing that the girl needs to be protected longer. Many girls become angry over this and feel that it is old-fashioned, unnecessarily restrictive, and a sign of partiality on the part of the parents. In fact, many girls mature faster than their male counterparts, and ought to be allowed their freedom accordingly.

School problems and teens
Teachers are human beings. Each has a unique personality, style of teaching, strong and weak points. A twin or singleton may have a personality that conflicts with a teacher's. Many times I have heard teens complain that "I hate that teacher" or "I'm not going to work in that class because I don't like the teacher" or "that teacher hates me."

It is best to nip this problem in the bud. A three-way conference with the teen, the teacher and you may help clear the air. Teens are not alone in taking too personally what an adult in authority intends to get across. Many of us feel that another's approach is designed to "get" us. We all make mistakes in assuming what the other person's motive is. Sometimes teachers make the same kinds of assumptions regarding the teenager's motives. By discussing the problem and bringing it out in the open, one may cause a more mature and productive relationship to grow. If the problem seems insoluble and the personality conflict too deeply entrenched, then a change of class and teacher may be indicated. Whether both twins should be transferred depends on their individual relationships with that teacher.

By high school, many children do not want parents to interfere in their problems because they feel they should be old enough to solve them themselves. Some will not even discuss what happens at school (although they need to be encouraged to do so). The important thing to keep in mind is the education. I encourage the teen to be "selfish" by getting as much out of a class or subject as possible, in spite of a poor relationship with the teacher; also, to avoid overreacting and personalizing. I point out that the teacher, being human, has a personal life with problems, needs and frustrations, just as the teen does.

We have to be able to assess how much stress our teenagers can tolerate; when we feel that point has been reached, then we intervene. To allow a school problem to go on endlessly can lead to dropping out or to a serious emotional complication.

Driving and teenagers

While states have minimum age standards for acquiring or applying for driver permits, we should remember that these are strictly legal requirements and have nothing to do with the individual's maturity level or ability to handle responsibility. The law sets the legal age, but it is up to the parents to determine the emotional age. It is up to the teens to demonstrate their maturity.

It is not uncommon to see one twin more than ready to drive at the minimum legal age, while the other does not feel ready (or it may be obvious to the parent that this twin is not ready). Again, we have a situation in which one twin may resent the other's advantage. By emphasizing readiness, we can discuss the criteria or objectives that must be met before the permit is obtained. Driver education classes, either through school or privately, provide excellent experiences; along with good grades, they also often enable the teen driver to qualify for lower insurance rates. If such classes are not available, or are too expensive, a patient parent may well make an excellent teacher; but sometimes a less emotionally involved adult may be better!

If teens responsibly carry out their school work and chores at home, get home on schedule, and reliably communicate their whereabouts, then the chances are they are ready to drive. If a teen is erratic, unpredictable, and does not handle responsibility at school or home, then it would be wiser to wait. Insurance company statistics suggest that teenagers are a very high risk group. Although their reflexes are very quick and they should theoretically be among the best drivers (and many of them are), their judgment, experience, and impulse control sometimes lag behind.

Depriving your teens of driving privileges when they break rules, slip grades, or commit driving infractions may be a very appropriate action to take. However, taking the car keys away should not be used as a weapon or threat for every misdeed; the teen may begin to see the car as a yo-yo and may retaliate, or may even lose interest in driving, thus depriving mother of a valued helper.

Keep them busy!

What do you do with 13- to 15-year-old twins in the summer? They are too old to play all day and too young for work permits, in most areas. Some are ambitious and seek their own work without our assistance or suggestions—they are probably in the minority. So here are some suggestions that may be helpful in making the summer or after-school hours more productive and enriching:

- Plan ahead. Make a list of possible employment opportunities. Some stores will hire younger teens for routine jobs—sweeping, bagging groceries, restaurant work, car washing, yard work, crop harvesting, etc. Encourage them to make contact early, well before school is out, so that they do not have to compete with the horde.
- Contact the state employment opportunity office. Some states have job banks, others have "Dial-a-Teen" agencies which call upon teens to do odd jobs for individuals who phone in requests.
- Sometimes twins will work together in their own business—lawn work, window washing (something most housewives hate to do), or house-, yard- and pet-sitting while neighbors or friends are on vacation.
- Baby-sitting or child care in groups. Two resourceful teenage girls set up a morning play period for children. They used their back yard and had approximately 12 youngsters over every morning. They planned and organized games, activities, and even a circus—and, in the process, not only made some cash, but learned a great deal about younger children.
- If no other paying opportunities are available, maybe mom and dad can provide a few—fences need painting, gardens need weeding, garages need to be cleaned, etc.
- Volunteer work can be an excellent alternative for several reasons. Teens need to be busy to keep from being bored, watching endless television, or becoming withdrawn. It is simply a matter of statistical probability that when kids get together for periods of increasing time with no real goal or activity, the chances of getting into trouble increase fantastically. Also, many young teens have led relatively sheltered lives. Volunteer work offers a variety of opportunities to learn about the community and to serve. Volunteering can open their eyes to the problems of the truly disadvantaged, those with health problems, physical deformities, the aged, the blind, deaf, retarded, or emotionally disturbed. The teenagers thus gain in maturity and in appreciation for their own blessings. Several twins I know locally work as hospital volunteers and as day care assistants; some are involved in park and recreation work and with ecology-oriented clean-up programs.
- By 13 or 15, most have had camping experiences, if they are at all interested, so that may be old hat. But being an assistant counselor or helper may be possible.

Teenage boozers

We all probably had a beer or two in high school. This may be a fashionable way to be part of a group, to rebel by doing the forbidden, or simply to experiment. After all, the teenage period is preparatory for adulthood and many like to prepare early!

Generally, unless it contradicts the family religious or moral values, there may be less trouble with teenagers sneaking out and drinking experimentally or excessively if alcohol is used sensibly and in moderation at home. Children may be allowed to sip a bit of wine on a special occasion (wine drinking is very common with children in Europe), or to share a gulp now and then of mom or dad's beer. In this way, the need to rebel by using alcohol may be deflated. We often see those who are raised to believe that alcohol is evil become more serious and determined drinkers than those who are raised in more relaxed atmospheres.

This can be a very complex and sensitive area which each family has to handle the way it feels is best. There is a balance to be struck. On the one hand, it is against the law to serve alcohol to minors, and as a rule parents should not encourage the breaking of a law; on the other hand, overzealousness and prohibition can develop an unnecessary need for, or curiosity about, alcohol because it has become such a taboo. Most parents whose children have gone through the drinking problem stage have suggested it is better to allow some leeway at home in order to lessen the chances of drinking and driving and other serious consequences of teenage drinking.

The drug problem

Although the drug scene has changed over the years, it is still with us and is likely to be with us for some time. Why does one 19-year-old fraternal twin girl make a beautiful adjustment to college and preparation for a professional career, while her sister becomes a junkie? The answer to this question is complex, but there are family dynamics which some of us feel contribute to drug use.

These girls were the youngest of four children in the family. The parents were middle class, the father had a stable income and was able to provide amply for the family's needs. There was nothing in the parents' personalities to suggest that they were poor or bad or selectively harsh to the drug addicted twin. Cindy, the college student, was the quicker, the more independent, and perhaps the leader of the two. Cathy, the heroin addict, was the more dependent, slower to achieve the developmental landmarks (walking, talking, toilet training, etc.), but was still within normal limits. Mother always felt a need to compensate for Cathy's deficiencies by spending more time, encouraging more, and in some respects developing a strong dependency attachment. The girls were sent to small private schools, always in the same classes. They dressed alike (even though fraternal) and enjoyed the same friends. When it came time for college, they went their separate ways. Cindy had the capacity to withstand the separation from twin and family, while Cathy fell apart emotionally. She became involved in a number of friendships with young men, looking for acceptance, love, and a chance to fulfill her dependency needs. All were catastrophic liaisons. She began experimenting with a variety of drugs in order to feel better and more secure, finally hitting upon heroin and, intermittently, speed. Counseling had no effect, but hospitalization finally led to her rehabilitation.

It would be oversimplifying to say that the problems Cathy endured were due to an overly protective mother, or to being dressed like her twin, or to being in the same class, or any of those particulars. But what we can say is that given her innate personality predisposition, given the family constellation and make-up of the parents, the school environment, and different college milieus—all these factors in combination probably contributed to Cathy's problem.

Serious drug abusers frequently come from broken homes, where emotional needs have not been met, where there is a chaotic history and emotional instability is prevalent. There is frequently very poor communication between addicts and their family, siblings and peers. Sometimes, the peer group pull is so strong that it overrides good parental influence.

When teenagers find it difficult to understand their parents, and when they feel that they do not understand, they feel alienated or separated and perhaps like strangers in their own home. This feeling of alienation may carry over to school, where, because their needs are not being met, they feel that they no longer belong. There may be a progression of the teenager dropping out of his family, then school, then community institutions such as church, scouts, and the like, and finally dropping out altogether. It is difficult to reach young people who are well along the road to alienation, and this is why we like to counsel them before the process has taken too heavy a toll.

Why drugs? Perhaps because we are such a medicine-oriented population. We are bombarded with television commercials dramatizing the importance of continued well-being and the need to avoid discomfort at all costs. Therefore, most family medicine chests are well-stocked arsenals. Parents take medicines for a variety of discomforts—hay fever, common cold symptoms, headaches, stomachaches, specific pain; to alleviate tension or sluggishness, to increase wakefulness, to reduce weight—as well as to treat very complex legitimate problems such as epilepsy, diabetes, heart disease, etc.

Identical twin boys (14 years old) used marijuana every weekend because "it makes us feel good, and besides, there is nothing else to do." Acceptance by a peer group and being governed by the "pleasure principle" were factors in this case. More advanced drug users seem to reveal a truly hedonistic approach: pleasure for pleasure's sake and "don't worry about tomorrow or the consequences." Other young people, finding themselves unhappy and in a purposeless existence, take drugs for lack of anything better to do. To them, it is a form of Russian Roulette. The most commonly used drug continues to be marijuana. Its effects are similar to alcohol: it reduces inhibitions, allows the individuals to feel more relaxed, more open, more spontaneous, while slowing reacting time and interfering with judgment or common sense. Continued use reduces incentive, drive, motivation, and interferes with problem-solving skills and, in some cases, produces paranoid states (increased suspiciousness).

My approach to teenagers who use drugs is not to wave the red flag or play a typical parental role, which they feel infringes on their rights, but rather to present them with the facts or reality:

- The use of drugs is against the law and, in many communities, a felony. The implications of this may be more far-reaching than teenagers realize, when they later go to apply for certain jobs requiring security checks. They may thus be limited for the rest of their lives.
- We do not know the full story as to what effect many of the drugs will have over a long period of time. I do not exaggerate or distort, but I provide as much updated factual material as possible.
- And, perhaps most importantly, I question this need for artificial crutches. Why can't they feel good enough in and of themselves, and have sufficient self-respect to make dependence on such artificial means unnecessary. Why can't they learn to live with themselves and with others and to enjoy the world around them—including music, the arts, and life in general—rather than leaning on something phony.

Treatment for drug abusers is varied. Your family doctor may be a good resource to advise you on the availability of resources. In some areas, there are specific treatment centers for those dependent on drugs. In others, existing facilities are expanding their resources to provide help. There may be individual, group, or family therapy, substitute family living arrangements, institutionalization, hospitalization, detoxification, and other withdrawal programs. When teenagers are able to define who they are, where they are going, what they want from life (that is, when they resolve the identity problem), and when they can feel some self-respect and gain some confidence in their roles, as well as becoming more confident in relating to others, they may not then need to continue to use drugs.

Teen sex
Entire books have been written on this subject. This is one of those areas in which parental values and standards may not be adopted easily by the teen. The new morality, permissiveness, let's-do-our-own-thing-as-long-as-it-doesn't-infringe-on-anyone's-rights, are attitudes expressed quite commonly today, not only by teens, but by adults as well. Statistically, the number of teens below 18 who are ready to accept the consequences of becoming involved sexually is probably as small as it always has been. And this is generally the approach I use with teens who discuss their sexual activities as though they were talking about going ice skating—I give them the facts and confront them with some of the potential consequences of their behavior.

Dropping out
One reason young people drop out of school is that they feel that the curriculum does not meet their needs and is irrelevant. In many respects, high school curricula have not changed appreciable for the past 100 years. Many young people fail to see the need for taking courses that have no immediate selling power. College-bound students generally accept their course of study at face value because admission to a university depends on completing it. But those students who plan to stop with their high school diploma, or to go on for vocational training, often have a legitimate gripe when it comes to the rather narrow class schedule with which they are faced. They eventually drop out because they see no meaning in it.

Then, there are those who feel rejected, misunderstood and alienated, and focus these feelings on the school. These are the youngsters who say, in effect, "Stop the world, I want to get off." These are the individuals whose emotional needs have not been met and who have experienced a serious breakdown in communication with both the family and the school personnel.

In my experience, it is rare for two twins to drop out unless economic factors are at work. If one drops out it will probably be the more rebellious of the two, the one who has chosen the "independent" role. The more conforming of the two, the one whose assumed role it is to please the parents and to achieve, generally continues with an education. As in the example of the drug abusing twin, we often find, in families with more than one child, that the children assume roles that appear to them as mutually exclusive. That is, if one is the superachiever, then another can't be; that role has been taken. One child may become a sports fan or athlete. Another may become active in music—and another may enjoy a role as rebel.

The teenage years can be happy years and should be a stimulating and challenging experience for both teens and their parents. By increasing our sensitivities as parents, by providing good examples, by sharing our thoughts, feelings and ideas, and by putting ourselves in the place of our teenagers, we can hope to avoid many of the pitfalls discussed in this chapter.

Organizations

The Center for Study of Multiple Birth (CSMB) is a public charity organized to stimulate and foster medical and social research in the area of multiple births. For more information, contact CSMB, Suite 464, 333 E. Superior St., Chicago, IL 60611, or call 312-266-9093.

Center for Loss in Multiple Birth Inc. (CLIMB) is a non-profit organization offering a newsletter, support and information resources for parents who have experienced the death of one, both or all of their children during a twin or higher-order multiple pregnancy, at birth or during infancy. For more information, write to CLIMB, P.O. Box 91377, Anchorage, AK 99509, or call 907-222-5321, e-mail: climb@pobox.alaska.net.

International Twins Association Inc. (ITA) is a non-profit organization promoting the spiritual, intellectual and social welfare of twins throughout the world. ITA holds its annual convention every Labor Day. For more information, contact ITA, c/o Lynn Long or Lori Stewart, 6898 Channel Road, NE, Minneapolis, MN 55432, or call 612-571-3022, e-mail: ITAConvention@aol.com, Web: www.intltwins.org.

Mothers of Supertwins (MOST) is a non-profit organization that serves the needs of families expecting multiples or those already the parents of triplets, quadruplets or quintuplets. For further information on MOST, write to P.O. Box 951, Brentwood, NY 11717, or call 631-859-1110, or web: www.mostonline.org.

Multiple Births Foundation provides professional support to families with twins and higher-order births through study days and newsletters, and by serving as a resource center. For more information, contact Multiple Births Foundation, Queen Charlotte's and Chelsea Hospital, DuCane Road, London, England, W12 0HS, or call 0208-383-3519, or e-mail: info@multiplebirths.org.uk, web: www.multiplebirths.org.uk.

The National Organization of Mothers of Twins Clubs Inc. (NOMOTC) is a non-profit nationwide network of parents of multiples clubs that shares information, concerns and advice, and focuses on education, support and research. Its annual convention is held in July. For more information, write to NOMOTC, P.O. Box 438, Thompson Station, TN 37179-0438, or call 877-540-2200, web: www.nomotc.org.

Multiple Births Canada is a non-profit organization whose purpose is to act as a general information source and liaison between parents and agencies, health caregivers and educators. For more information about the organization and its annual convention, write to Multiple Births Canada, P.O. Box 432, Wasaga Beach, Ontario, Canada L0L 2P0, or call 705-429-0901, or e-mail: office@multiplebirthscanada.org, web: www.multiplebirthscanada.org.

Special Children is a non-profit support network for parents raising multiples with special needs. For more information about available services and the organization's quarterly newsletter, contact Sharon Devo, P.O. Box 8193, Bartlett, IL 60103, or call 630-213-1630, or e-mail at spclchldrn@aol.com.

The Triplet Connection is a non-profit agency founded as a support service for expectant and new parents of larger multiples. The organization provides preterm-birth prevention information as well as networking opportunities. For more information, write to The Triplet Connection, P.O. Box 99571, Stockton, CA 95209, call 209-474-0885, or e-mail: TC@tripletconnection.org, web: www.tripletconnection.org.

Twin Hope Inc. is a non-profit organization providing service to families, educating the public and broadening the awareness of twin to twin transfusion syndrome and other twin-related diseases. For more information, write Twin Hope Inc., 2592 W. 14th Street, Cleveland, OH 44113, or call 502-243-2110.

Twinless Twins International is a membership of twins of all ages whose co-twins are deceased or terminally ill. For more information, contact Twinless Twins International, P.O. Box 980481, Ypsilanti, MI 48198, 880-205-8962, e-mail: contact@twinlesstwins.org, web: www.twinlesstwins.org.

The Twin to Twin Transfusion Syndrome (TTTS) Foundation Inc. is a non-profit organization dedicated to providing educational, emotional and financial support to families and caregivers before, during and after pregnancies diagnosed with TTTS. For more information, write Mary Slaman-Forsythe, Executive Director, 411 Longbeach Parkway, Bay Village, OH 44140, call 440-899-8887, or e-mail at info@tttsfoundation.org, web: www.tttsfoundation .org.

Twin Services is a non-profit agency offering a variety of services to help parents cope and to enable health and family service providers to meet the needs of families with multiples. For more information, send a self-addressed, stamped envelope to Twin Services, P.O. Box 10066, Berkeley, CA 94709, or call the TWINLINE 510-524-0863, or e-mail at twinservices@Juno.com.

The Twins Foundation is a non-profit membership organization and a research information center on twins that includes a national twin registry and a quarterly newsletter. For information, contact The Twins Foundation, P.O. Box 6043, Providence, RI 02940-6043, or call 401-729-1000, or e-mail at twinsfdn@aol.com, web: www.twins-foundation.com.

Recommended Reading

Albi, Linda, et al. *Mothering Twins: From hearing the news to beyond the terrible twos.* New York: Simon & Schuster, A Fireside Book, 1993.

Dodson, Fitzhugh. *How to Parent.* New York: NAL/Dutton, 1971.

Editors of Twins Magazine. *The Twinship Sourcebook: Your guide to understanding multiples.* Overland Park, Kan.: TWINS Magazine, 1992.

Gehman, Betsy Holland. *Twins: Twice the trouble, twice the fun.* Philadelphia: Lippincott, 1965.

Graham, Phyllis. *Care and Feeding of Twins.* New York: Harper, 1955.

Ilg, Francis L., et al. *Child Behavior: from the Gesell Institute of Human Behavior.* New York: Harper & Row, 1981.

Manginello, Frank, and Theresa Fay DiGeronimo. *Your Premature Baby: Everything you need to know about childbirth, treatment, and parenting of premature infants.* New York: John Wiley & Sons, 1991.

Noble, Elizabeth. *Having Twins: A parent's guide to pregnancy, birth, and early childhood.* 2nd ed. Boston: Houghton Mifflin Co., 1991.

Novotny, Pamela Patrick. *The Joy of Twins and Other Multiple Births.* Revised ed. New York: Crown Trade Paperbacks, 1994.

Rothbart, Betty. *Multiple Blessings: From pregnancy through childhood, a guide for parents of twins, triplets, or more.* New York: Hearst Books, 1994.

Scheinfeld, Amram. *Twins and Super-Twins.* New York: Viking Penguin, 1973.

Unell, Barbara C., and Jerry Wyckoff. *Twenty Teachable Virtues: Practical ways to pass on lessons of virtue and character to your children.* New York: The Berkley Publishing Group, A Perigee Book, 1995.

Wyckoff, Jerry, and Barbara C. Unell. *Discipline Without Shouting or Spanking: Practical solutions to the most common preschool behavior problems.* New York: Meadowbrook Press, 1984.

Wyckoff, Jerry, and Barbara C. Unell. *How to Discipline Your Six to Twelve Year Old ... Without Losing Your Mind.* New York: Doubleday, 1991.